Second Financial Narrative Processing Workshop (FNP 2019)

Turku, Finland
30 September 2019

ISBN: 978-1-5108-9441-9

FNP 2019

Proceedings of the Second Financial Narrative Processing Workshop (FNP 2019)

30 September, 2019
Turku University
Turku, Finland

Preface

Welcome to the Second Financial Narrative Processing Workshop (FNP 2019) held at NoDaLiDa 2019 in Turku, Finland. Following the success of the First FNP 2018 at LREC'18, Japan, we have had a great deal of positive feedback and interest in continuing the development of the financial narrative processing field. This prompted us to hold a training workshop in textual analysis methods for financial narratives that was oversubscribed showing that there is an increasing interest in the subject. As a result, we were motivated to organise the Second Financial Narrative Processing Workshop, FNP 2019. The workshop will focus on the use of Natural Language Processing (NLP), Machine Learning (ML), and Corpus Linguistics (CL) methods related to all aspects of financial text mining and financial narrative processing (FNP). There is a growing interest in the application of automatic and computer-aided approaches for extracting, summarising, and analysing both qualitative and quantitative financial data. In recent years, previous manual small-scale research in the Accounting and Finance literature has been scaled up with the aid of NLP and ML methods, for example to examine approaches to retrieving structured content from financial reports, and to study the causes and consequences of corporate disclosure and financial reporting outcomes. One focal point of the proposed workshop is to develop a better understanding of the determinants of financial disclosure quality and the factors that influence the quality of information disclosed to investors beyond the quantitative data reported in the financial statements. The workshop will also encourage efforts to build resources and tools to help advance the work on financial narrative processing (including content retrieval and classification) due to the dearth of publicly available datasets and the high cost and limited access of content providers. The workshop aims to advance research on the lexical properties and narrative aspects of corporate disclosures, including glossy (PDF) annual reports, US 10-K and 10-Q financial documents, corporate press releases (including earning announcements), conference calls, media articles, social media, etc.

For FNP 2019 we collaborated with Fortia Financial Solutions, a French based company specialised in Financial Investment and Risk management who will work with us on organising a shared task on automatic detection of financial documents structure as part of FNP 2019. http:// fortia.fr/

We accepted 11 submissions of which are 5 main workshop papers and 6 shared task papers, all papers accepted for oral presentation in the workshop. The papers cover a diverse set of topics in financial narratives processing reporting work on financial reports from different stock markets around the globe presenting analysis of financial reports. The quantity and quality of the contributions to the workshop are strong indicators that there is a continued need for this kind of dedicated Financial Narrative Processing workshop. We would like to acknowledge all the hard work of the submitting authors and thank the reviewers for the valuable feedback they provided. We hope these proceedings will serve as a valuable reference for researchers and practitioners in the field of financial narrative processing and NLP in general.

Dr Mahmoud El-Haj, General Chair, on behalf of the organizers of the workshop   September 2019

Organising Committee

- Mahmoud El-Haj, Lancaster University, UK
- Paul Rayson, Lancaster University, UK
- Steven Young, Lancaster University, UK
- Houda Bouamor, Carnegie Mellon University in Qatar, Qatar
- Sira Ferradans, Fortia Financial Solutions, France
- Catherine Salzedo, Lancaster University, UK

Program Committee

- Antonio Moreno Sandoval (UAM, Spain)

- Catherine Salzedo (LUMS, Lancaster University, UK)

- Denys Proux (Naver Labs, Switzerland)

- Djamé Seddah (INRIA-Paris, France)

- Eshrag Refaee (Jazan University, Saudi Arabia)

- George Giannakopoulos (SKEL Lab – NCSR Demokritos, Greece)

- Haithem Afli (Cork Institute of Technology, Ireland)

- Houda Bouamor (Carnegie Mellon University in Qatar, Qatar)

- Mahmoud El-Haj (SCC, Lancaster University, UK)

- Marina Litvak (Sami Shamoon College of Engineering, Israel)

- Martin Walker (University of Manchester, UK)

- Paul Rayson (SCC, Lancaster University, UK)

- Simonetta Montemagni (Istituto di Linguistica Computazionale – ILC, Italy)

- Sira Ferradans (Fortia Financial Solutions, France)

- Steven Young (LUMS, Lancaster University, UK)

Programme

09:00	09:15	Opening Remarks and Introduction to FNP

Session 1   **Financial Narrative Processing Papers**

09:15	09:40	Introduction to Financial Narrative Processing Tools and Resources Mahmoud El-Haj
09:40	10:05	Tone Analysis in Spanish Financial Reporting Narratives Antonio Moreno-Sandoval, Ana Gisbert, Pablo Alfonso Haya, Marta Guerrero and Helena Montoro
10:05	10:30	Coffee Break
10:30	10:55	Automated Stock Price Prediction Using Machine Learning Mariam Mokalled, Wassim El-Hajj and Mohamad Jaber
10:55	11:20	Utilizing Pre-Trained Word Embeddings to Learn Classification Lexicons with Little Supervision Frederick Blumenthal and Ferdinand Graf
11:20	11:45	Towards Unlocking the Narrative of the United States Income Tax Forms with Natural Language Processing Esme Manandise
11:45	12:10	Active learning for financial investment reports Sian Gooding and Ted Briscoe
12:10	13:30	Lunch Break

Session 2   **FinTOC Shared Task**

13:30	13:45	The FinTOC-2019 Shared Task: Financial Document Structure Extraction Remi Juge, Imane Bentabet and Sira Ferradans
13:45	14:00	UWB@FinTOC-2019 Shared Task: Financial Document Title Detection Tomas Hercig and Pavel Král
14:00	14:15	FinTOC-2019 Shared Task: Finding Title in Text Blocks Hanna Abi Akl, Anubhav Gupta and Dominique Mariko
14:15	14:30	FinDSE@FinTOC-2019 Shared Task Carla Abreu, Henrique Cardoso and Eugénio Oliveira

14:30	14:45	Daniel@FinTOC-2019 Shared Task : TOC Extraction and Title Detection
		Emmanuel Giguet and Gaël Lejeune
14:45	15:00	Finance document Extraction Using Data Augmented and Attention
		Ke Tian and Zi Jun Peng
15:00	15:05	Closing Remarks

Table of Contents

Finance document Extraction Using Data Augmentation and Attention

Ke Tian
OPT Inc, Tokyo, Japan
tianke0711@gmail.com

Zijun Peng
Harbin Institute of Technology (Weihai),China
2986320586@qq.com

Abstract

This paper mainly describes the aiai that the team submitted to the FinToc-2019 shared task. There are two tasks. One is the title detection task from non-titles in the finance documents. Another one is the TOC (table of contents) prediction from the finance PDF document. The data augmented and attention-based LSTM and BiLSTM models are applied to tackle the title-detection task. The experiment has shown that our methods perform well in predicting titles in finance documents. The result achieved the 1st ranking score on the title detection leaderboard.

1 Introduction

In the finance field, a great number of financial documents are published in machine-readable formats such as PDF file format for reporting firms' activities and financial situations or revealing potential investment plans to shareholders, investors, and the financial market. Official financial prospectus PDF documents are the documents that describe precisely the characteristics and investment modalities of investment funds. Most prospectuses are published without a table of contents (TOC) to help readers navigate within the document by following a simple outline of headers and page numbers and assist legal teams in checking if all the contents required are fully included. Thus, automatic analyses of prospectuses by which to extract their structure are becoming increasingly more vital to many firms across the world. Therefore, the second Financial narrative processing (FNP) workshop is the first proposal of the FinTOC-2019 shared task to focus on the financial document structure extraction (Rmi Juge, 2019). Two tasks are contained in the FinTOC-2019 task.

Title detection (task 1): This is a two-label classifications task that detects text block as titles or non-titles in the financial prospectuses document. For example, in the training data, there are about 9 fields:

(1) text blocks: a list of strings computed by a heuristic algorithm; the algorithm segments the documents into homogeneous text regions according to given rules.

(2) begins_with_numbering : 1 if the text block begins with a numbering such as 1., A, b), III., etc.; 0 otherwise

(3) is_bold: 1 if the title appears in bold in the PDF document; 0 otherwise

(4) is_italic: 1 if the title is in italic in the pdf document; 0 otherwise

(5) is_all_caps: 1 if the title is all composed of capital letters; 0 otherwise

(6) begins_with_cap: 1 if the title begins with a capital letter; 0 otherwise

(7) xmlfile: the xmlfile from which the above features have been derived

(8) page_nb: the page number in the PDF where appears the text bock

(9) label: 1 if text line is a title, 0 otherwise

There are eight fields, which are the same as the training data in the test data except the label field. The goal of this task is to detect the text blocks as titles or non-titles.

TOC generation (task2): this subtask will predict the TOC from the PDF document. There are annotated TOCs in the XML format in the document structure as well as PDFs. The XML file is composed of TOC-titles with three attributes:

(1) title: a title of the document

(2) page: the page number of the title

(3) matter_attrib: whether the title appears on the front page, the body, or the back matter of the documents.

There are about five levels of titles that can be inferred from the hierarchy of the XML file. The training documents are the same as those for the title detection sub-task. The test documents are the same as the training data with the title labels. The PDF and XML documents are provided in the test data. The goal of this task is to generate the TOC XML file of the test data.

In this research, we first recreate the training and test data using data augmentation to be new training and test data for task1, and then we use attention-based LSTM and BiLSTM modes to detect the title in task1. Section 2 explains the details of our methods. Section 3 shows experimental configurations and discusses the results. Then, we conclude this paper in Section 4.

2   Methods

The structure of the proposed method for tackling with task 1 is shown in Figure 1. The recreation of training, test data and word embedding using data augmentation are described in Section 2.1. The attention of the long short-term memory (LSTM) (Sepp and JRgen, 1997) model and BiLSTM (Mike and Kuldip, 1997) are described in Section 2.2, and the ensemble result is presented in Section 2.3.

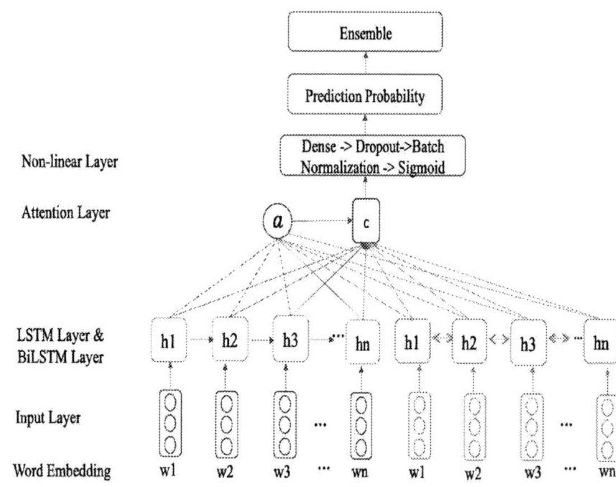

Figure 1: The Structure of attention-based LSTM and BiLSTM

2.1   Data Augmentation

The train and test data are provided in the title detection task, except the label field. There are eight fields used to predict the label. Before using these data for prediction, the train and test data are recreated. The procedure for recreating the new training and test data is shown in Figure 2.

As with the text blocks, we used the NLTK first to tokenize the text, and then all the tokenized words were converted to be lower. Secondly, we

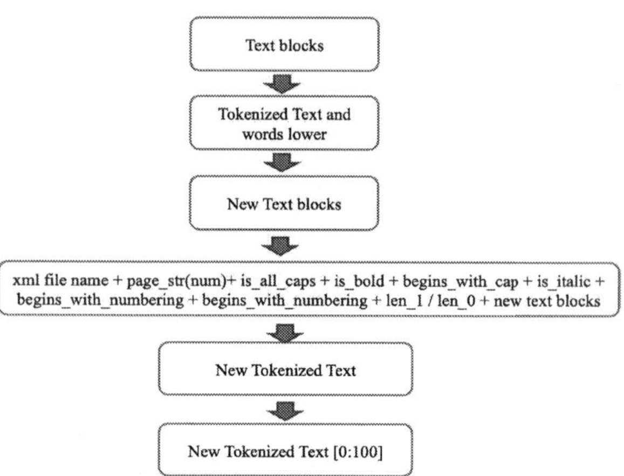

Figure 2: The procedure of data augmentation

computed the length of all text blocks labeled 1, namely the title in the train data. We observed the length of all title text blocks is less than 60. Therefore, if the length of text block is more than 60, the len_1 word is added before the new text block; otherwise the len_0 is added. Thirdly, the begins_with_numbering is added if the value of this field is 1 before len_1 or len_0, the same as is_italic, begins_with_cap, is_bold, is_all_caps words are added subsequently if the field value is 1. Finally, the page number, and xml file name of text blocks are added in the front of the previous new text blocks. For example, take the first text block DB PWM I in the train data to explain the procedure. The other seven fields are as follows: begins_with_numbering (0), is_bold (1), is_italic (0), is_all_caps (1), begins_with_cap (1), xmlfle (LU0641972152-LU0641972079_English_2015_DBPWMIGlobalAllocationTracker-.xml), page_nb (1). Based on the data augmentation procedure, the new text block is LU0641972152-LU0641972079_English_2015_DBPWMIGlobalAllocationTracker.xml page_1 is_all_caps is_bold begins_with_cap len_0 db pwm i.

Word embedding is the foundation of deep learning for natural language processing. We use the new train and test text data to train the word embedding. In the recreated text data, there are recreated sentences with 14,285 unique token words from the training, dev, and test data. The CBOW model (Tomas et al., 2013) is taken to train word vectors for the recreated text block, and the word2vec dimension is set to 100.

2.2 Attention-based LSTM and BiLSTM Model

After the data augmentation is completed, we only take the previous 120 words of each text block as the input sentence. In the structure of the proposed model as shown in Fig. 1, the LSTM and BiLSTM layer, the embedding dimension and max word length of word embedding are set to be 100 and 120, respectively, as the embedding dimension. The embedding layer of the word embedding matrix is an input layer of LSTM, and the size of the output dimension is 300.

Through the task train data, we observe that some keywords could help indicate the label of the text block. For example, most of title text blocks have the following features: len_0, begins_with_cap, is_bold, is_all_caps. hus, some keywords in the new data have more importance to predict the label of the text block. Since the attention mechanism can enable the neural model to focus on the relevant part of your input, such as the words of the input text (Tian and Peng, 2019), attention mechanism is used to solve the task. In this paper, we mainly use the feed-forward attention mechanism (Colin and Daniel, 2015). The attention mechanism can be formulated with the following mathematical formulation:

$$e_t = a(h_t), \alpha_t = \frac{exp(e_t)}{\sum_{k=1}^{T} -exp(e_k)}, c = \sum_{k=1}^{T} \alpha_t h_t \tag{1}$$

In the above mathematical formulation, a is a learnable function and only depend on h_t. The fixed length embedding c of the input sequence computes with an adaptive weighted average of the state sequence h to produce the attention value.

As the non-linear layer, the activation function is to dense the output of the attention layer to be 256 dimensions, and by using the dropout rate of 0.25, the output result after the dropout rate will be batch normalization. Finally, the sigmoid activation function that will dense the dimension of batch normalization input will be the length of the label as the final output layer.

2.3 Ensemble Result

In the model training stage, the 10-fold cross-validation is used to train the deep attention model for predicting the test data. We sum 10 folds of predict probability and get the mean value of 10 folds for the final predict probability result. In the

Team name	Score
Aiai_1	0.9818997315023511
Aiai_2	0.9766402240293054
UWB_2	0.9723895009266195
FinDSE_1	0.9700572855958501
FinDSE_2	0.9684006306179805
UWB_1	0.9653446892789734
Daniel_1	0.9488117489093626
Daniel_2	0.9417339436713312
YseopLab_1	0.9124937810249167
YseopLab_2	0.9113421072180891

Table 1: Leader board of title detection task.

title detection task, two results for each language are submitted: one result is based on the word embedding of attention-based LSTM, and the other result is based on word embedding of the BiLSTM.

3 Experiment and Result

In the experiment, the proposed deep attention model has been implemented in the task. We have submitted two results. One result is attention-based LSTM. The other one is the attention-based BiLSTM. The evaluation metric used for this title detection task is the weighted F1 score. The final result of attention-based LSTM and BiLSTM ranking 1st and 2nd in the leader board are shown in Table 1.

4 Conclusion

We have described how we tackle title detection in the FinToc-2019 shared task. Firstly, we augmented the text block and added another 7 fields to recreate the new training and test data. Then, the attention-based LSTM and BiLSTM models are experimented on. The experimental result showed that the proposed model could effectively solve the goal of the task and achieve a very good performance in carrying out this task.

For future work, more models or methods will be implemented for the task. Moreover, we have planned to tackle Task 2.

References

Raffel Colin and P. W. Ellis Daniel. 2015. Feed-forward networks with attention can solve some long-term memory problems. arXiv:1512.08756.

Schuster Mike and K. Paliwal Kuldip. 1997. Bidirectional recurrent neural networks. *IEEE TRANSACTIONS ON SIGNAL PROCESSING*, 45:2673–2681.

Sira Ferradans Rmi Juge, Najah-Imane Bentabet. 2019. The fintoc-2019 shared task: Financial document structure extraction. In *The Second Workshop on Financial Narrative Processing of NoDalida 2019*, Turku, Finland.

Hochreite Sepp and A Schmidhuber JRgen. 1997. Long short-term memory. *Neural Computation*, 9:1735–1780.

Ke Tian and Zijun Peng. 2019. aiai at finnum task: Financial numeral tweets fine-grained classification using deep word and character embedding-based attention model. In *The 14th NTCIR Conference*.

Mikolov Tomas, Sutskever Ilya, Chen Kai, Corrado Greg, and Dean Jeffrey. 2013. Distributed representations of words and phrases and their compositionality. arXiv:1310.4546.

Utilizing Pre-Trained Word Embeddings to Learn Classification Lexicons with Little Supervision

Frederick Blumenthal
d-fine GmbH
frederick.blumenthal@d-fine.de

Ferdinand Graf
d-fine GmbH
ferdinand.graf@d-fine.de

Abstract

A lot of the decision making in financial institutions, regarding particularly investments and risk management, is data-driven. An important task to effectively gain insights from unstructured text documents is text classification and in particular sentiment analysis. Sentiment lexicons, i.e. lists of words with corresponding sentiment orientations, are a very valuable resource to build strong baseline models for sentiment analysis that are easy to interpret and computationally efficient. We present a novel method to learn classification lexicons from a labeled text corpus that incorporates word similarities in the form of pre-trained word embeddings. We show on two sentiment analysis tasks that utilizing pre-trained word embeddings improves the accuracy over the baseline method. The accuracy improvement is particularly large when labeled data is scarce, which is often the case in the financial domain. Moreover, the new method can be used to generate sensible sentiment scores for words outside the labeled training corpus.

1 Introduction

A vast amount of information in business and especially in the finance area is only available in the form of unstructured text documents. Automatic text analysis algorithms are increasingly being used to effectively and efficiently gain insights from this type of data. A particularly important text analytics task is document classification, i.e. the task to assign a document to a category within a set of pre-defined categories. For example, annual reports, news articles and social media services like twitter provide textual information that can be used in conjunction with structured data to quantify the creditworthiness of a debtor. To give another example, intelligent process automation may require the categorization of documents

to determine the process flow. In both cases, sound text classification algorithms help saving costs and efforts.

To tackle the problem of document classification, classical methods combine hand-engineered features, e.g. word-count based features, n-grams, part-of-speech tags or negations features, with a non-linear classification algorithm such as Support Vector Machine (Joachims, 1998). A detailed survey of classical sentiment analysis models, a special case of text classification, has been compiled by Pang et al. (2008) and Liu (2012).

Since the reign of deep learning, various neural network architectures such as convolutional neural networks (CNN) (Kim, 2014; dos Santos and Gatti, 2014), character level CNNs (Zhang et al., 2015), recursive neural networks (Socher et al., 2013), recurrent neural network (RNN) (Wang et al., 2015; Liu et al., 2016) and transformers (Vaswani et al., 2017) have been utilized in text classification models to yield state-of-the-art results.

Recently, a steep performance increase has been achieved by very large pre-trained neural language models such as ELMo (Peters et al., 2018), BERT (Devlin et al., 2018), XLNet (Yang et al., 2019) and more (Howard and Ruder, 2018; Radford et al., 2018; Akbik et al., 2018). These models generate powerful text representations that can be either used as context-aware word embeddings or the models can be directly fine tuned to specific tasks.

One disadvantage of these pre-trained language models, however, is the high demand of memory and computing power, e.g. a sufficiently large GPU to load the large models. In finance, many documents that can be the subject of text classification applications (e.g. annual reports or legislative documents), are very large, so that the computational cost becomes very relevant. Another disadvantage is that because of their complexity, many state-of-the-art deep learning models are hard to interpret and it is very difficult to retrace the model predictions. Model interpretability, however, seems to be particularly important for many financial institutions and interpretable models with transparent features are often favored over more complex models even if the complex models are more accurate.

A powerful resource for building *interpretable* text classification models are classification lexicons and in particular sentiment lexicons. A sentiment lexicon is a list of words (or n-grams) where each word is assigned a sentiment orientation. The sentiment orientation can be binary, i.e. each word in the lexicon is labeled as *positive* or *negative*, or continuous where a continuous sentiment score is assigned to the words (e.g. in the interval [-1, 1]). More generally, a classification lexicon is a list of words where each word is assigned a vector with one score for each class.

Sentiment lexicons have been an integral part of many classical sentiment analysis classifiers (Mohammad et al., 2013; Vo and Zhang, 2015). Approaches based on sentiment lexicons seem to be particularly popular in the finance domain (Kearney and Liu, 2014). In addition, it has been shown that even modern neural network models can profit from incorporating sentiment lexicon features (Teng et al., 2016; Qian et al., 2016; Shin et al., 2016). Using classification lexicon features can be thought of as a way of inducing external information that has been learned from different data sets or compiled by experts.

Three approaches to sentiment lexicon generation are usually distinguished in the literature, namely the manual approach, the dictionary-based approach and the corpus-based approach, see for example (Liu, 2012, Chapter 6). A popular finance specific lexicon has been compiled by Loughran and McDonald (2011) from 10-K fillings , but see also the General Inquirer (Stone et al., 1962) and the Subjectivity Lexicon (Wilson et al., 2005).

Fairly recently, models have been designed to generate sentiment lexicons from a labeled text corpus. In many cases distant supervision approaches are employed to generate large amounts of labeled data. For example, Mohammad and Turney (2013) compiled a large twitter corpus where noisy labels are inferred from emoticons and hashtags. Count-based methods such as pointwise mutual information (PMI) generate sentiment scores for words based on their frequency in positive and negative training sentences (Mohammad and Turney, 2013; Kiritchenko et al., 2014).

A more direct approach to learn sentiment lexicons from labeled corpora is to use supervised machine learning. The basic idea is to design a text classification model that contains a parametrized mapping from word token to sentiment score and an aggregation of word-level sentiment scores to document scores. The parametrized mapping which yields the sentiment lexicon is learned during training. Severyn and Moschitti (2015) proposed a linear SVM model and showed that the machine learning approach outperforms count-based approaches. A simple linear neural network model has been proposed by Vo and Zhang (2016). A similar model with a slightly more complex neural network architecture is used by Li and Shah (2017). They use data from StockTwits, a social media platform designed for sharing ideas about stocks, which they also use to generate sentiment-specific word embeddings.[1] Pröllochs et al. (2015) design a linear model and add L1 regularization to optimally control the size of the sentiment lexicons.

We see two main challenges for the generation of new domain specific classification lexicons via a pure supervised learning approach.

- The generation of robust classification lexicons requires large amounts of supervised training data. Manual labeling of data is very expensive and a distant (or weak) labeling approach may not be possible for all applications.

- Using small or medium size supervised training data, one may encounter many words at prediction time that are not part of the training corpus.

---

[1]The objective of sentiment-specific word embeddings, first proposed by Maas et al. (2011), is to map words (or phrases) close to each other if they are both semantically similar and have similar sentiment. A sentiment lexicon could be considered as one-dimensional or two-dimensional word embeddings.

To tackle these problems, we propose a novel supervised method to generate classification lexicons by utilizing unsupervised data in the form of pre-trained word embeddings. This approach allows to build classification lexicons with very small amounts of supervised data. In particular, it allows extending the classification lexicon to words outside the training corpus, namely to all words in the vocabulary of the pre-trained word embedding.

The remainder of this paper is structured as follows. Section 2 gives a short introduction to supervised learning of classification lexicons in general and then introduces the novel model extension to utilize pre-trained word embeddings. We show empirically in Section 3 that the use of pre-trained word embeddings improves prediction accuracy and generates better classification lexicons. The accuracy improvement is particularly large for small training data sets. In addition, we show that the model generates sensible word-level class scores for words that are not part of the training data. For the experiments we use the popular SST-2 sentiment analysis dataset which is part of the GLUE benchmark and a new dataset of manually labeled financial newspaper headlines. In Section 4 we describe how a modification of the proposed method can be applied to hierarchical (multi-level) document classification and supervised sentence highlighting in large documents.

2   Methodology

The goal is to learn a classification lexicon, that is, for a given set of word tokens (or n-grams) $\mathcal{D} = \{x^{(l)}\}_{l=1}^{L}$, the task is to learn a domain specific function $s : \mathcal{D} \rightarrow \mathbb{R}^{C}$ that assigns each token a vector of class scores. The resulting classification lexicon $\mathcal{L}$ is then defined as the set of tuples consisting of tokens $x^{(l)}$ and corresponding C-dimensional class scores s_l,

$$\mathcal{L} = \{(x^{(1)}, s_1), \dots, (x^{(L)}, s_L)\}. \quad (1)$$

In the specific case of sentiment analysis, the function s may be two-dimensional with channels for positive and negative sentiment or higher-dimensional in order to represent fine-grained nuances of sentiment.

For supervised learning of the classification lexicon, a data set with labeled text sentences is used, i.e. a data set $D = \{(t_n, y_n)\}_{n=1}^{N}$ that consists of sentences (or other pieces of text) t_n with corresponding class label $y_n \in \{1, \dots, C\}$. In this setting, the overall idea is to design a classification model that consists of an elementwise mapping s from word token to word-level class scores and a function f that aggregates the word class scores to sentence-level class probabilities,

$$\boldsymbol{p}(t) = \boldsymbol{f}\left(\boldsymbol{s}(x_1), \boldsymbol{s}(x_2), \dots, \boldsymbol{s}(x_{|t|})\right), \quad (2)$$

with $\boldsymbol{p} \in [0, 1]^{C}$ and $|t|$ denotes the number of words in sentence t. The objective is to learn the functions s and f such that the model as accurately as possible predicts the sentence class labels of the training data. The learned function s then yields the mapping to generate the classification lexicon.

Note that this is a special case of a more general class of hierarchical (multi-level) text classification models that generate class scores for low-level segments and then aggregate these scores to produce document-level classifications. This is discussed in more detail in Section 4.

In order to assure that the learned function s actually produces sensible word-level class scores, the following two conditions have to be fulfilled.

- The function $s(x)$ that maps a token to a class score must not depend on context, i.e. each word token in the lexicon must be mapped to a unique class score value. If the mapping was context dependent, then a single word might be assigned to multiple class scores.

- The aggregation function f must be designed such that the predicted sentence-level class probabilities have a clear dependence on the word-level class scores. In particular, an increase in a certain word-level class score must ceteris paribus increase the sentence-level probability for this class (more than for any other class). That is, for each sentence t, each class $c' \neq c \in \{1, \dots, C\}$ and each token $x \in t$,

$$\frac{\partial p_c(t)}{\partial s_c(x)} > \frac{\partial p_{c'}(t)}{\partial s_c(x)}. \quad (3)$$

To design a model instance in this general setting

one has to specify the mapping $s(x)$ and the function f from Eq. (2) such that the above conditions are satisfied.

2.1 Baseline

Arguably the simplest instance of the described approach, which we use as our baseline model, is to use as function s a direct mapping and as aggregation function f a simple averaging followed by a softmax function. Very similar models have been proposed in previous works (Severyn and Moschitti, 2015; Pröllochs et al., 2015; Vo and Zhang, 2016).

Representing the word tokens x as one-hot vectors, the direct mapping s from word token to word-level class scores can be formulated as a simple matrix-vector multiplication,

$$s(x) = Sx, \tag{4}$$

where S is the class score embedding matrix of dimensionality $C \times L$. The columns of matrix S give the classification lexicon, i.e. the lth column gives the class scores for token x^l. The word-level class scores are then averaged to compute sentence level class scores,

$$z(t) = \frac{1}{|t|} \sum_{x \in t} s(x) \tag{5}$$

that are finally normalized to yield probabilities,

$$p_c(t) = \frac{e^{z_c(t)}}{\sum_{c'=1}^{C} e^{z_{c'}(t)}}. \tag{6}$$

The only parameters of the model are the elements of the class score matrix S, that is, the elements of the classification lexicon. To tune the model parameters we minimize the average cross-entropy over the training data,

$$L_{CE}(D|S) = -\frac{1}{N} \sum_{n=1}^{N} \sum_{c=1}^{C} y_{nc} \log p_c(t_n) + \lambda |S|_1 \tag{7}$$

where $L1$ regularization is added as proposed by Pröllochs et al. (2015). Is is known that $L1$ regularization tends to drive model parameters to zero which in this case reduces the size of the classification vocabulary. This behavior can be desirable because many words in the training data (e.g. stop words) are not expected to carry any sensible class score.

2.2 New approach

In the baseline model, a direct mapping from word token to word-level class score is learned from scratch for every word token. In particular, no prior knowledge about semantic relationships between word tokens is considered in the model. Semantic similarity between words can be captured very well by pre-trained word embeddings such as *word2vec* or *GloVe*. Therefore, we propose a classification lexicon model that is build on top of word embeddings. This way, prior knowledge is induced into the model that has been previously learned from a very large and representative unsupervised corpus. This should be particularly useful when learning a classification lexicon from a small supervised corpus.

For the token-level score function s from Eq. (2) a two-step function is designed that first maps the word token to its word vector and then transforms the word vector to a token class score,

$$s(x) = \bar{s}(w(x)) \tag{8}$$

where $w(x)$ is the word embedding of token x with dimensionality E. The aggregation function is the same as in the baseline model, that is, the class score of a sentence is modeled as the average over the word scores which are then normalized by a soft-max function, see Eq. (5) and (6).

The function $\bar{s} : \mathbf{R}^E \to \mathbf{R}^C$ is modeled as a multilayer fully connected neural network with ReLU activations,

$$h^{(1)} = \text{ReLU}\left(W^{(1)} w(x)\right)$$
$$h^{(2)} = \text{ReLU}\left(W^{(2)} h^{(1)}\right)$$
$$\vdots$$
$$h^{(H)} = \text{ReLU}\left(W^{(H)} h^{(H-1)}\right)$$
$$s = W^{(final)} h^{(H)}. \tag{9}$$

We choose all of the H hidden layers to be of some fixed length I, the word-level class scores s have length C. This gives a total of $I\left(E + (H-1)I + C\right)$ parameters. A high-level sketch of the classification lexicon model is shown in Figure 1. It should be noted that the same function $\bar{s}$ is applied independently to each word token. This can be efficiently implemented e.g. by a convolutional layer with kernel size 1.

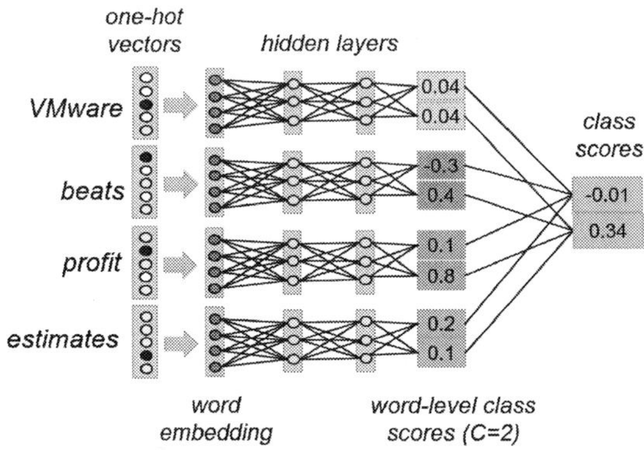

Figure 1: Sketch of the word embeddings based classification lexicon model for a dictionary of $L = 5$ words, a $E = 4$ dimensional word embedding, C=2 classes, $H = 2$ hidden layers with $I = 3$ hidden units. To predict the class probabilities of a piece of text, the word-level class scores are computed from pre-trained word embeddings via a set of of linear transformations followed by rectifiers. The class prediction for the text is computed as the average over word-level class scores.

Since the word embeddings in the model are trained in an unsupervised fashion it is possible that words with very different true class scores are assigned very similar word vectors. Fine-tuning the word embeddings during training could help to separate words with similar pre-trained embedding but different true class scores. However, we decide not to fine-tune the word embeddings during training, because we want to apply the mapping $\bar{s}$ to words that are not part of the training data. Moreover, fine-tuning the word embeddings, which would introduce an additional set of $E \cdot L$ model parameters, did not improve the model accuracy in the experiments.

3 Experiments

The purpose of the proposed classification model is to generate powerful application specific classification lexicons and we want to show that the new model generates better lexicons than the baseline model. To this end, we train both models on two binary sentiment analysis datasets and compare the test set accuracy as a proxy for the classification lexicon quality. Since the new word-embedding based model and the baseline model contain the same aggregation function, any improvement in model predictions must result from the word-level classification scores, i.e. the learned classification lexicons.

The first dataset that we use for the evaluation is the SST-2 dataset (Socher et al., 2013) that contains binary labeled movie reviews. This well-known dataset is publicly available and part of the GLUE benchmark (Wang et al., 2018). The second dataset, which we call *FNHL*, consists of financial news headlines that have been manually labeled by experts. Table 1 shows simple examples from both datasets and Table 2 gives basic dataset statistics. It should be emphasized that the proposed model is not restricted to binary classification problems and could also be applied to multi-class datasets.

FNHL
(+) *French rail network gets three offers for new line*
(-) *Google, Facebook to face tougher EU privacy rules*

SST-2
(+) *the movie exists for its soccer action and its fine acting*
(-) *the plot grinds on with yawn-provoking dullness*

Table 1: Examples from the SST-2 and FNHL datasets.

Dataset	mean($|t|$)	N	$|V|$	$|V_{w2v}|$
SST-2	19	9613	16182	14826
FNHL	10	2792	5885	4664

Table 2: Average sentence length (mean($|t|$)), total dataset size (N), vocabulary size ($|V|$) and vocabulary that is contained in word2vec ($|V_{w2v}|$). Computed on the pre-processed datasets.

Both the baseline and the new model are implemented as neural networks and optimized via the Adam optimizer. For the baseline model dropout regularization is applied to the word level class scores and for the new model dropout is applied before the rectifiers. The new model is implemented with pre-trained word2vec word embeddings. For words that are not contained in word2vec the embedding is set to a vector of zeros. Since the embedding model can always be refined based on an unlabeled domain-specific corpus, one can ensure that the embedding model contains the relevant vocabulary. The SST-2 dataset is provided with a train/dev/test split which is used in our experiments whereas for the FNHL dataset nested cross-validation is used. The dev set is used for early stopping and to evaluate model hyperparameters via grid-search. The optimal hyperparameters are provided in Table 7 in the appendix.

3.1 Model Accuracy

Table 3 shows that the new model outperforms the baseline model on both datasets which means that the new model generates better sentiment lexicons. As an additional experiment we implement the new model with ELMo embeddings which further increases the accuracy on the SST-2 dataset by 3.7%. Since ELMo embeddings are context-dependent this model does not yield a fixed sentiment lexicon but instead yields a mapping from sentence-token pair to sentiment scores.

To put the accuracy of the baseline model and the new classification lexicon model into perspective, we show in Table 3 the accuracy on SST-2 for several GLUE benchmark models as well as recent state-of-the-art models as reported on the official GLUE website, see `https://gluebenchmark.com/leaderboard`. CBoW denotes an average bag-of-words model using GloVe embeddings, GenSen (Subramanian et al., 2018) denotes the GLUE benchmark sentence representation model with best overall score and InferSent (Conneau et al., 2017) denotes the GLUE benchmark sentence representation model with best SST-2 score. For these models a mapping from sentence representation to class scores was trained. Our new classification lexicon model outperforms the baseline models CBoW and GenSen whereas InferSent achieves slightly better accuracy.

The BiLSTM model with ELMo embeddings and attention (BiLSTM+ELMo+Attn) achieves only 2.6% higher accuracy than NewElmo, i.e. a simple mapping from ELMo to token level class scores. As expected, the popular BERT model and XL-Net, the currently best performing model on the SST-2 task, achieve much better accuracy than our proposed classification lexicon model. It should be emphasized, however, that the purpose of the proposed model is not to achieve state-of-the-art accuracy but to generate powerful sentiment lexicons. Therefore, the most relevant result is that the proposed model outperforms the baseline classification lexicon model which shows that the new model generates better sentiment lexicons.

To evaluate the dependency between training set size and model accuracy, the experiments are repeated with subsampled SST-2 training sets, see Figure 2. For small training sets, the new model

	FNHL	SST-2
Baseline	77.4 (75.0, 78.4)	82.5
New	82.8 (82.1, 83.9)	84.1
NewElmo	-	87.8
CBoW	-	80.0
GenSen	-	83.1
InferSent	-	85.1
BiLSTM+ELMo+Attn	-	90.4
BERT	-	94.9
XLNet	-	96.8

Table 3: Accuracy of the baseline and new classification lexicon models. NewElmo denotes the implementation of the new model with ELMo embeddings (which does not yield a lexicon). For comparison, the accuracy on the SST-2 task are shown for the GLUE baseline models CBoW, GenSen, InferSent and BiLSTM+ELMo+Attn as well as the popular BERT model and the currently best performing model XLNet.

outperforms the baseline model by a large margin. For example, with 1% of training samples (69 samples) the new model achieves 69% accuracy compared to 54% for the baseline model and with 5% of training samples (346 samples) the new model yields an accuracy of 79% compared to 66% for the baseline model.

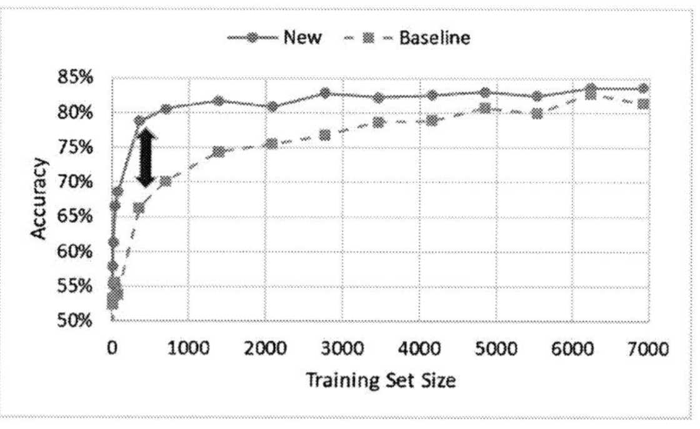

Figure 2: Prediction accuracy on the SST-2 dataset with training set subsampled to different sizes. For small training set sizes the new model significantly outperforms the baseline model.

3.2 Sentiment Lexicons

After a quantitative comparison of the new and baseline classification lexicon models, we now want to take a qualitative look at the generated lexicons. Table 4 shows the tails of the sentiment lexicons as generated by the new model on the FNHL and SST-2 datasets. The well-known domain-specific character of sentiment lexicons is apparent.

Positive words	Negative words
SST-2	
melds, combines, marvelously, enhances, hearts, sublimely, breathtaking, wonderfully, engagingly, supple, winningly, searing, enables, heartwarming, integrates, captures, mesmerizing, infuses, masterly, explores	charmless, ineffective, garbled, misfire, itis, useless, uncreative, dumped, uninspiring, overinflated, unimaginative, unfocused, incoherent, drowned, unambitious, pointless, halfhearted, suffers, faulty, squandering
FNHL	
wins, bt, topping, airshow, turbines, awarded, selected, supercomputer, clinch, debut, paves, beats, tops, inks, secures, buoyed, success, boosted, driverless	violated, violations, falls, lapses, delisted, underreporting, violating, fined, plummet, threatened, misled, sues, fining, drags, infringe, delisting, halts, breaches, fines, censures

Table 4: Example of words in the sentiment lexicons trained on the FNHL and SST-2 datasets using the word-embedding based model.

Table 5 shows the largest word-level sentiment score differences between baseline and new model. Qualitatively, the new model seems to generate more sensible sentiment scores. For the comparison, the two-channel word-level scores are first transformed to a scalar score, $\frac{s_{pos}-s_{neg}}{s_{pos}+s_{neg}}$, and normalized to $[-1, 1]$.

word	Base	New	word	Base	New
ineffective	0.0	-1.0	melds	0.0	0.7
dumped	0.0	-0.9	seagal	-0.6	0.0
garbled	-0.2	-1.0	sweetest	-0.3	0.3
uncreative	-0.1	-0.9	supple	0.0	0.6
itis	-0.2	-1.0	pay	-0.7	-0.1
overinflated	-0.1	-0.9	spry	-0.1	0.4
atrociously	0.0	-0.7	enables	0.0	0.6
uninspiring	-0.2	-0.9	queen	-0.6	-0.1
moldy	0.0	-0.7	convenient	-0.4	0.1
counterproductive	-0.1	-0.7	windtalkers	-0.5	0.0
unambitious	-0.2	-0.8	sheridan	-0.5	0.0
miserably	0.1	-0.6	guess	-0.6	-0.1
knockoff	-0.1	-0.8	dynamic	-0.4	0.2
untalented	-0.1	-0.7	equilibrium	-0.6	0.0

Table 5: Largest differences between sentiment lexicons generated by the baseline and new model.

3.3 Lexicon Extension

By design, the baseline model can only generate word-level class scores for words that are contained in the training corpus. The new model on the other hand learns an application specific mapping from word embedding to word-level class scores. This makes it straight forward to generate class-scores for words outside the training corpus. To evaluate this property we apply the learned mapping (from SST-2 dataset) to a subset of the pre-trained word vectors in word2vec. The word2vec set is filtered to lowercase 1-grams, i.e. phrases are excluded. This leaves a total of 180000 words which is more than 10 times the number of words in the SST-2 training set vocabulary.

Table 6 shows the most positive and most negative sentiment words when applied to the 180000 tokens in word2vec. Most of the words look sensible, which shows that it is possible to generate sentiment scores for words that are not contained in the training corpus. Arguably, this ability to generate scores for unseen words is the reason why the new model significantly outperforms the baseline model on very small training sizes as shown in Figure 2. Of course, the extension of the lexicons also generates poor scores for some words. Qualitatively unplausible words are underlined in Table 6. In general during all sentiment lexicon model evaluations we got the impression that negative words have better quality than positive words.

Positive words
equips, revolutionizing, amazes, reconnects, delighting, soothes, optimizes, prayerfully, backflip, accelerations, empowers, nourishes, maximizes, flyby, centenarians, transfixing, juxtaposes, exhilaratingly, purifies, frugally, caresses, predeceased, glistened, livability, centenarian, policyowners, gratified, securityholders, astound, electrifying, sacraments, equanimity, synchronizes

Negative words
uncompetitive, unproductive, overstocking, misaligned, misconfigured, mistyped, spams, fritz, untargeted, scrapyard, clunked, uninformative, slouching, unworkable, knockoffs, unmarketable, mixup, ineffectively, misdirected, forlornly, misspell, polluter, overleveraged, overwrites, dumper, plagiarized, unemployable, unimpressive, defective, overloaded, flunky, laminitis

Table 6: Words in the word2vec set (filtered for lowercase 1-grams) with most positive and most negative sentiment as generated by the proposed model that has been trained on the SST-2 training set. Most word sentiments are plausible, unplausible words are underlined.

4 Hierarchical Document Classification

In some document classification tasks in the finance domain one deals with very long documents, such as annual reports or legislative documents, that may consist of more than 100 pages. In order to make model predictions more interpretable it would be desirable that the predictions on document level can be retraced to the sentence (or paragraph) level. One advanced approach to achieve this level of locality is to incorporate sentence-level attention in the document-level model, see for example (Yang et al., 2016). For each sentence the attention function indicates how relevant the sentence is for the document-level model prediction. This makes the model predictions more interpretable, i.e. the analyst could better understand the model predictions by looking at the most relevant sentences.

A somewhat simpler approach is to build a model that generates class scores per sentence and then aggregates these scores to document-level class scores. By designing the aggregation such that the document-level scores are in a direct relationship to the sentence-level scores, one can train a joint model for document-level classification that – at the same time – generates sentence-level predictions. This approach is analogous to the classification lexicon model where word-embeddings are replaced by sentence representations. See Figure 3 for a sketch of the model. The sentence representation model is arbitrary and could be for example a pre-trained language model such as BERT or a jointly trained BiLSTM pooling of ELMo embeddings.

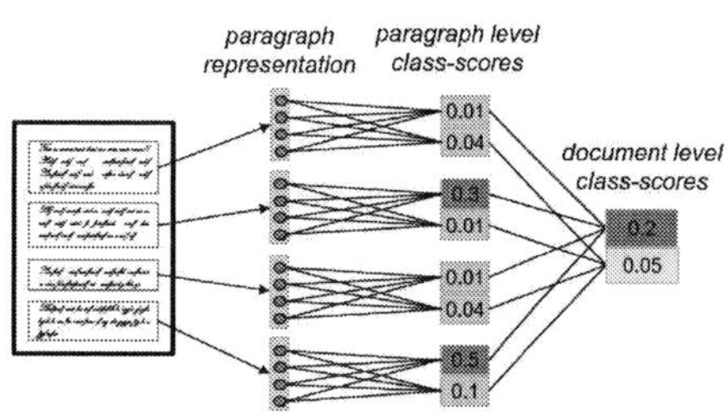

Figure 3: Sketch of a basic architecture for hierarchical document classification. Sentence representations can be computed for example by average pooling all word embeddings in the sentence. Sentence representations are mapped by a parametric function to yield the sentence score for each class. Finally, aggregation (e.g. simple averaging) of the sentence-level class scores yields the document level scores.

The described approach localizes model predictions to the sentence level and thereby makes predictions on large documents interpretable. In addition, the approach can be utilized as a supervised method to highlight important sentences in a document. For example, a financial institution that has to process a large number of annual reports or fund reports can employ such methods to point the analyst to the important parts of the document. In such an application the final document prediction may not be relevant primarily, but the highlighting via sentence level scores is important. Highlighting approaches that we currently see in practice are mostly based on unsupervised text-summarization algorithms such as LexRank (Erkan and Radev, 2004) , which also determines an importance score on sentence-level based on non-parametrical similarity measures and graph-methods, and can also be used in conjunction with our approach.

During our literature review on hierarchical document classification, no model was found that is comparable to the approach described above. However, the general idea to design a joint model for document-level classification that generates sentence-level predictions as a byproduct is not new and has been proposed for example by Yessenalina et al. (2010).

5   Conclusion

This paper presents a novel supervised method to generate classification lexicons that utilizes unsupervised learning in the form of pre-trained word embeddings. The method allows to build classification lexicons, e.g. sentiment lexicons, from very small amounts of labeled data and the model allows to extend the lexicons to words that are not contained in the training corpus. This is very relevant for applications in the financial and compliance area, where labeled data is very sparse and usually very unbalanced. In addition, in these areas cross-institutional data pooling is usually not possible for data protection reasons, and data encryption would render the data useless.

It was shown that using the proposed method with context-dependent word embeddings such as ELMo yields powerful word-level features.[2]

To improve the overall classification lexicon

---

[2]Implementing the approach with context-dependent word-embeddings yields a context-dependent mapping from words to class scores and thus does not produce a classification lexicon.

model the knowledge distillation approach (Ba and Caruana, 2014; Hinton et al., 2015) could be used where a simple model is trained on the raw predictions of a more complex model. In our case the new classification lexicon model could be trained for example on the class scores (scores before softmax function) of BERT or XLNet. The potential improvements of distilling knowledge from BERT to simple neural networks has been demonstrated recently by Tang et al. (2019). The classification lexicon model could be further improved, e.g. by using phrases or n-grams, and escaping named entities.

In Section 4 a modified version of the classification lexicon model is described that can be used for supervised sentence highlighting in large documents. We would like to investigate the performance of this model in future work.

References

Alan Akbik, Duncan Blythe, and Roland Vollgraf. 2018. Contextual string embeddings for sequence labeling. In *Proceedings of the 27th International Conference on Computational Linguistics*, pages 1638–1649.

Jimmy Ba and Rich Caruana. 2014. Do deep nets really need to be deep? In *Advances in neural information processing systems*, pages 2654–2662.

Alexis Conneau, Douwe Kiela, Holger Schwenk, Loic Barrault, and Antoine Bordes. 2017. Supervised learning of universal sentence representations from natural language inference data. *arXiv preprint arXiv:1705.02364*.

Jacob Devlin, Ming-Wei Chang, Kenton Lee, and Kristina Toutanova. 2018. Bert: Pre-training of deep bidirectional transformers for language understanding. *arXiv preprint arXiv:1810.04805*.

Günes Erkan and Dragomir R. Radev. 2004. Lexrank: Graph-based lexical centrality as salience in text summarization. *Journal of Artificial Intelligence Research*, 22:457–479.

Geoffrey Hinton, Oriol Vinyals, and Jeff Dean. 2015. Distilling the knowledge in a neural network. *arXiv preprint arXiv:1503.02531*.

Jeremy Howard and Sebastian Ruder. 2018. Universal language model fine-tuning for text classification. In *Proceedings of the 56th Annual Meeting of the Association for Computational Linguistics (Volume 1: Long Papers)*, volume 1, pages 328–339.

Thorsten Joachims. 1998. Text categorization with support vector machines: Learning with many relevant features. In *European conference on machine learning*, pages 137–142. Springer.

Colm Kearney and Sha Liu. 2014. Textual sentiment in finance: A survey of methods and models. *International Review of Financial Analysis*, 33:171–185.

Yoon Kim. 2014. Convolutional neural networks for sentence classification. *arXiv preprint arXiv:1408.5882*.

Svetlana Kiritchenko, Xiaodan Zhu, and Saif M Mohammad. 2014. Sentiment analysis of short informal texts. *Journal of Artificial Intelligence Research*, 50:723–762.

Quanzhi Li and Sameena Shah. 2017. Learning stock market sentiment lexicon and sentiment-oriented word vector from stocktwits. In *Proceedings of the 21st Conference on Computational Natural Language Learning (CoNLL 2017)*, pages 301–310.

Bing Liu. 2012. Sentiment analysis and opinion mining. *Synthesis lectures on human language technologies*, 5(1):1–167.

Pengfei Liu, Xipeng Qiu, and Xuanjing Huang. 2016. Recurrent neural network for text classification with multi-task learning. *arXiv preprint arXiv:1605.05101*.

Tim Loughran and Bill McDonald. 2011. When is a liability not a liability? textual analysis, dictionaries, and 10-ks. *The Journal of Finance*, 66(1):35–65.

Andrew L Maas, Raymond E Daly, Peter T Pham, Dan Huang, Andrew Y Ng, and Christopher Potts. 2011. Learning word vectors for sentiment analysis. In *Proceedings of the 49th annual meeting of the association for computational linguistics: Human language technologies-volume 1*, pages 142–150. Association for Computational Linguistics.

Saif M Mohammad, Svetlana Kiritchenko, and Xiaodan Zhu. 2013. Nrc-canada: Building the state-of-the-art in sentiment analysis of tweets. *arXiv preprint arXiv:1308.6242*.

Saif M Mohammad and Peter D Turney. 2013. Crowdsourcing a word–emotion association lexicon. *Computational Intelligence*, 29(3):436–465.

Bo Pang, Lillian Lee, et al. 2008. Opinion mining and sentiment analysis. *Foundations and Trends® in Information Retrieval*, 2(1–2):1–135.

Matthew E Peters, Mark Neumann, Mohit Iyyer, Matt Gardner, Christopher Clark, Kenton Lee, and Luke Zettlemoyer. 2018. Deep contextualized word representations. *arXiv preprint arXiv:1802.05365*.

Nicolas Pröllochs, Stefan Feuerriegel, and Dirk Neumann. 2015. Generating domain-specific dictionaries using bayesian learning. In *ECIS*.

Qiao Qian, Minlie Huang, Jinhao Lei, and Xiaoyan Zhu. 2016. Linguistically regularized lstms for sentiment classification. *arXiv preprint arXiv:1611.03949*.

Alec Radford, Karthik Narasimhan, Tim Salimans, and Ilya Sutskever. 2018. Improving language understanding by generative pre-training. *URL https://s3-us-west-2. amazonaws. com/openai-assets/research-covers/language-unsupervised/language_ understanding_paper. pdf.*

Cicero dos Santos and Maira Gatti. 2014. Deep convolutional neural networks for sentiment analysis of short texts. In *Proceedings of COLING 2014, the 25th International Conference on Computational Linguistics: Technical Papers*, pages 69–78.

Aliaksei Severyn and Alessandro Moschitti. 2015. On the automatic learning of sentiment lexicons. In *Proceedings of the 2015 Conference of the North American Chapter of the Association for Computational Linguistics: Human Language Technologies*, pages 1397–1402.

Bonggun Shin, Timothy Lee, and Jinho D Choi. 2016. Lexicon integrated cnn models with attention for sentiment analysis. *arXiv preprint arXiv:1610.06272.*

Richard Socher, Alex Perelygin, Jean Wu, Jason Chuang, Christopher D Manning, Andrew Ng, and Christopher Potts. 2013. Recursive deep models for semantic compositionality over a sentiment treebank. In *Proceedings of the 2013 conference on empirical methods in natural language processing*, pages 1631–1642.

Philip J. Stone, Robert F. Bales, J. Zvi Namenwirth, and Daniel M. Ogilvie. 1962. The general inquirer: A computer system for content analysis and retrieval based on the sentence as a unit of information. *Behavioral Science*, 7(4):484–498.

Sandeep Subramanian, Adam Trischler, Yoshua Bengio, and Christopher J Pal. 2018. Learning general purpose distributed sentence representations via large scale multi-task learning. *arXiv preprint arXiv:1804.00079.*

Raphael Tang, Yao Lu, Linqing Liu, Lili Mou, Olga Vechtomova, and Jimmy Lin. 2019. Distilling task-specific knowledge from bert into simple neural networks. *arXiv preprint arXiv:1903.12136.*

Zhiyang Teng, Duy Tin Vo, and Yue Zhang. 2016. Context-sensitive lexicon features for neural sentiment analysis. In *Proceedings of the 2016 Conference on Empirical Methods in Natural Language Processing*, pages 1629–1638.

Ashish Vaswani, Noam Shazeer, Niki Parmar, Jakob Uszkoreit, Llion Jones, Aidan N Gomez, Łukasz Kaiser, and Illia Polosukhin. 2017. Attention is all you need. In *Advances in Neural Information Processing Systems*, pages 5998–6008.

Duy-Tin Vo and Yue Zhang. 2015. Target-dependent twitter sentiment classification with rich automatic features. In *IJCAI*, pages 1347–1353.

Duy Tin Vo and Yue Zhang. 2016. Don't count, predict! an automatic approach to learning sentiment lexicons for short text. In *Proceedings of the 54th Annual Meeting of the Association for Computational Linguistics (Volume 2: Short Papers)*, volume 2, pages 219–224.

Alex Wang, Amapreet Singh, Julian Michael, Felix Hill, Omer Levy, and Samuel R Bowman. 2018. Glue: A multi-task benchmark and analysis platform for natural language understanding. *arXiv preprint arXiv:1804.07461.*

Xin Wang, Yuanchao Liu, SUN Chengjie, Baoxun Wang, and Xiaolong Wang. 2015. Predicting polarities of tweets by composing word embeddings with long short-term memory. In *Proceedings of the 53rd Annual Meeting of the Association for Computational Linguistics and the 7th International Joint Conference on Natural Language Processing (Volume 1: Long Papers)*, volume 1, pages 1343–1353.

Theresa Wilson, Janyce Wiebe, and Paul Hoffmann. 2005. Recognizing contextual polarity in phrase-level sentiment analysis. *Proc. of HLT-EMNLP-2005.*

Zhilin Yang, Zihang Dai, Yiming Yang, Jaime Carbonell, Ruslan Salakhutdinov, and Quoc V Le. 2019. Xlnet: Generalized autoregressive pretraining for language understanding. *arXiv preprint arXiv:1906.08237.*

Zichao Yang, Diyi Yang, Chris Dyer, Xiaodong He, Alex Smola, and Eduard Hovy. 2016. Hierarchical attention networks for document classification. In *Proceedings of the 2016 Conference of the North American Chapter of the Association for Computational Linguistics: Human Language Technologies*, pages 1480–1489.

Ainur Yessenalina, Yisong Yue, and Claire Cardie. 2010. Multi-level structured models for document-level sentiment classification. In *Proceedings of the 2010 Conference on Empirical Methods in Natural Language Processing*, pages 1046–1056. Association for Computational Linguistics.

Xiang Zhang, Junbo Zhao, and Yann LeCun. 2015. Character-level convolutional networks for text classification. In *Advances in neural information processing systems*, pages 649–657.

A Hyperparameters

The optimal model hyperparameters, see Table 7, are determined via grid search with evaluation on the respective dev set. The batch size is fixed to 100 and each model is trained until no further dev set accuracy is observed.

Model	Dataset	Hyperparameters	
Baseline	SST-2	LR	0.05
		d	0.8
		λ	10^{-6}
	FNHL	nested CV	
New	SST-2	LR	0.001
		d	0.7
		I	500
		H	3
	FNHL	nested CV	
NewElmo	SST-2	LR	0.001
		d	0.7
		I	500
		H	3

Table 7: Optimal hyperparameters for each model on the SST-2 dataset. For the FNHL dataset nested cross-validation is used. LR: learning rate for the Adam Optimizer, d: dropout rate, λ: L1 regularization strength, I: number of hidden units, H: number of hidden layers.

Automated Stock Price Prediction Using Machine Learning

Mariam Moukalled   Wassim El-Hajj   Mohamad Jaber
Computer Science Department
American University of Beirut
{mim23,we07,mj54}@aub.edu.lb

Abstract

Traditionally and in order to predict market movement, investors used to analyze the stock prices and stock indicators in addition to the news related to these stocks. Hence, the importance of news on the stock price movement. Most of the previous work in this industry focused on either classifying the released market news as (positive, negative, neutral) and demonstrating their effect on the stock price or focused on the historical price movement and predicted their future movement. In this work, we propose an automated trading system that integrates mathematical functions, machine learning, and other external factors such as news' sentiments for the purpose of achieving better stock prediction accuracy and issuing profitable trades. Particularly, we aim to determine the price or the trend of a certain stock for the coming end-of-day considering the first several trading hours of the day. To achieve this goal, we trained traditional machine learning algorithms and created/trained multiple deep learning models taking into consideration the importance of the relevant news. Various experiments were conducted, the highest accuracy (82.91%) of which was achieved using SVM for Apple Inc. (AAPL) stock

1   Introduction

The financial market is a dynamic and composite system where people can buy and sell currencies, stocks, equities and derivatives over virtual platforms supported by brokers. The stock market allows investors to own shares of public companies through trading either by exchange or over-the-counter markets. This market has given investors the chance of gaining money and having a prosperous life through investing small initial amounts of money, low risk compared to the risk of opening new business or the need of high salary career (Investopedia, July 2008). Stock markets are affected by many factors causing the uncertainty and high volatility in the market.

Although humans can take orders and submit them to the market, automated trading systems (ATS) that are operated by the implementation of computer programs can perform better and with higher momentum in submitting orders than any human. However, to evaluate and control the performance of ATSs, the implementation of risk strategies and safety measures applied based on human judgements are required. Many factors are incorporated and considered when developing an ATS, for instance, trading strategy to be adopted, complex mathematical functions that reflect the state of a specific stock, machine learning algorithms that enable the prediction of the future stock value, and specific news related to the stock being analyzed.

Several studies have been done on the topic of predicting stock price trends mainly for a daily timeframe, where models have been built integrating different sources of data such as news articles, twitter data, google and Wikipedia data. All these external factors when integrated with stock prices and stock technical indicators have shown the effect on stock price movements.

The stock market is considered a volatile market due to the external factors affecting its movements, dynamicity of the market and complexity of dimensionality which makes the prediction task of the trend/price of the stock a difficult and challenging task even with deep learning models (Singh, Aishwarya 2019). These external factors can be grouped into fundamental factors, technical factors and market sentiments as follows:

- Supply and demand. For example, if traders tend to buy this stock more than selling it, this will affect the price probably by rising since the demand will be more than the supply.

- Stock prices can have unexpected moves because of a single news which keeps a stock artificially high or low. Hence, investors cannot predict what will happen with a stock on a day-to-day basis. This is called market sentiment factors and they include company news, economy, and world events.
- Global economy. The flow of money and transactions is based on the economy of the traders which is affected by the economy of the country.
- Stock historical prices. Each stock has a range which tick data moves within, when looking into chart patterns and behavior of investors.
- Public sentiments and social media. A tweet from a president or an article release affects the price of the related stock(s). For example, an unofficial resignation of a CEO on twitter.
- Natural disasters. For example, the "haiti earthquake" that killed around 316,000 people affected the S&P index by going down 6.6% after 18 trading days.
- Earnings per share (EPS) is a fundamental factor that affects stock price. Investors tend to purchase stocks with high EPS since they know that they will gain substantial profits. The demand on this stock, the company management, the market sector dominance and the cyclical industry performance result in the movement of the stock price.
- Inflation and deflation are technical factors. Inflation means higher buy price and thus higher interest rates. This will result in a decrease of stock price. On the contrary, deflation means lower buy prices and thus lower profits and interest rate.

All these diverse factors and others affect price movements, leading to a difficulty in stock prediction. Researchers assume that market prediction does not exhibit random behavior (Schumaker, R. et al. 2009). Many publications have been done on the topic attempting to increase the accuracy of future price predictions. Mark L. et al. (1994) studied the influence of public information reported by Dow Jones and concluded that a direct relation does exists between released news articles and stock market activities.

News released related to an activity of a company results in assumptions for traders that will affect price movement. For instance, when positive news is released, traders tend to buy resulting in stock price increase. On the contrary, when negative news is released, traders tend to sell and thus pushing stock price to decrease. Although there is no doubt that news affect traders' actions, only few studies use the news factor in predicting price movement.

Different machine learning algorithms can be applied on stock market data to predict future stock price movements, in this study we applied different AI techniques using market and news data. This paper is arranged as follows. Section 2 provides literature review on stock market prediction. Section 3 details the data collection process, data +cleaning, and the ML models' design. Section 4 provides the experimental results, and section 5 concludes the paper and presents future work.

2 Related work and background

In the early research related to stock market prediction, Fama, E. F. (1970) proposed the Efficient Market Hypothesis (EMH) and Horne, J. C., & Parker, G. G. (1967) proposed the Random Walk theory. These theories proposed that market prices are affected by information other than historical prices and thus market price cannot be predicted.

The EMH theory suggests that the price of a stock depends completely on market information and thus any new information will lead to a price change as a reaction of the newly released information. This theory also claimed that stocks are always traded on their fair value, where traders cannot buy nor sell stocks in a special price undervalued or inflated and therefore the only way a trader can increase her profits is by increasing her risk. EMH discusses three different variations that affect market price: Weak Form, where only historical data is considered, semi- Strong Form, which incorporates current public data in addition to historical data, and Strong Form, which goes farther to incorporate private data. EMH states that any price movement is either a result of new released information or a random move that would prevent prediction models from success.

The Random Walk Hypothesis by Horne, J. C., & Parker, G. G. (1967) states that the stock prices are randomly changed and argue that past price movements are independent of current movements. This is slightly different from EMH as it focuses on short-term pattern of stock market.

Based on the above two hypotheses by Horne, J. C. et al. (1967) and Fama, E. F. (1970), the stock market will follow a random move and the accuracy of predicting such movement cannot exceeds 50%.

As opposed to these theories, many recent studies have shown that stock market price movement can be predicted to some degree. These studies depend on two different types of financial analysis to predict stock market prices:

- Fundamental Analysis: it is based on the health of the company and this includes qualitative and quantitative factors such as interest rate, return on assets, revenues, expenses and price to earnings among others. The aim of this analysis is to check the long-term sustainability and strength of the company for the purpose of long-term investment.
- Technical analysis: It is based on time series data. Traders analyze historical price movements and chart patterns and consider time as a crucial parameter in the prediction. Technical analysis can rely on three main keys: stock prices movement although many times the movement seems to be random, historical trends which are assumed to repeat as time passes, and all relevant information about a stock.

In most recent studies, different machine learning techniques have been used to predict stock prices. Machine learning was proven to be a good tool used in price predictions tasks due to the techniques it uses in analyzing data to drawing generalized pattern. Different machine learning models and risk strategies have been applied to stock market prediction task trying to predict mainly the direction of the price for different time frames and using different features that would affect market prices.

Arévalo, A. et al. (2016) used four main features as input to a Depp Neural Network (DNN) model. These features can be considered as technical analysis features for the stock market as they are based on mathematical calculations as described below:

- Log return: a finance term that represents the logarithmic difference between the close price at time t and close price at time t-1
- Pseudo-log-return: the logarithmic difference between average prices of consecutive minutes
- Trend Indicator: a linear model applied on 1-minute tick data to generate a linear equation with a certain slope. A negative slope implies a decrease in the price while a positive slope

implies an increase and a slope close to zero implies that the price is almost stable.

Arévalo, A. et al. 2016 formalize the input data as follows: the time feature which is included in the inputs as minutes and hours parameters, and a variable window size (n) which is used for the other inputs. Thus, the input file will include last n pseudo-log-return, last n standard deviations and last n trend indicators. The output of the model was "next one-minute pseudo-log-ret. Then after having the input data file ready, it was given to a DNN with one input layer, five hidden layers and one output layer. The data was fragmented into training and testing data. The model was trained during 50 epochs with different window sizes and the results show that window size 3 can show the best performance of the model with accuracy 66% and 0.07 MSE.

Weng, B. et al. (2017) attempted to predict one-day ahead price movement using disparate sources of data, where combining data from online sources with prices and indicators can enhance the prediction of the stock market state. This study was tested on Apple Inc. (APPL) stock information gathered over 3 years with multiple inputs and different output targets. The target was a binary value (0 or 1) which represent a fall or rise of variation between prices. Four datasets were gathered from disparate sources: first dataset includes the public information available at yahoo finance online for stock prices; second dataset includes number of unique page visits to Wikipedia per visitor per day; third dataset includes count of data published on google related to a company on a specific date; forth dataset includes three technical indicators (Stochastic Oscillator, Larry William, Relative Strength index) that represent the variation of stock price over time. Additional features were generated from the four datasets to provide a meaningful parameter for the model. Twenty features were selected as input. A common observation was drawn, that for any target, all the datasets were represented by at least one feature. Different AI techniques: Artificial Neural Network (ANN), Support Vector Machines (SVM) and Decision Trees (DT) were applied to predict stock price movement and compared to each other. After the evaluation on the three different models listed above, the output comparing open price of day i+1 to open price of day i achieves the best prediction accuracy with around 85% using SVM model.

Schumaker, R. P. et al. (2009) tried to predict direction of the price movement based on financial news. The study was done in 2009 as market prediction was and still facing difficulties due to the ill-defined parameters. In order to use the financial news articles in the prediction model, news should be represented as numerical value. Several techniques have been known to analyze articles related to certain stock to label these articles with sentiments or use them as vectors for the input features. These techniques could be bag of words, noun phrases, named entities and proper nouns. Proper noun technique is a combination of noun phrases and named entities. The proposed technique outperformed other techniques based on a comparison study.

AZFin Text is another system built by (Schumaker, R. P. et al 2009) that predicts price changes after 20 minutes of news release. The main component of this system is the financial news articles collected from yahoo finance and represented as noun phrases; all the collected noun phrases are represented as vector of binary values indicating the presence or absence of a phrase in the article. The second main component of this system is the stock price data collected in one-minute time frame. Then, the final major task after collecting the data and formalizing the inputs was building and training the AI model. To finalize the input of the model, stock price quotation at the same minute news was released, have been added to the input matrix, in addition to that +20 minutes price which will be the output of the system. The data was then fed to different models. Support Vector Regression (SVR) model was built to predict the price after 20 minutes of news release. Only the data during market time was included leaving 1 hour for opening of the market to show the effect of news released during the closure of the market. Moreover, a new constraint was added to the model where only one article could be used for 20 minutes. If two articles were released during the same 20-minute period, both will be discarded. The results show that the average directional accuracy established was 71.18%.

It is evident that released news and published articles affect the market. Most of the existing studies analyzing news rely on shallow features such as bag-of-words, named entities and noun phrases. A newer representation was introduced by (Ding, X. et al. 2014) which represents news as structured events to predict the daily stock price movement. Unlike the previous approaches, this representation can show the relation between events since representing phrases as vectors or bag of words cannot show the actor, action, and the actor which the action was applied on, thus trivial representations cannot show the relation between event and stock. To evaluate the performance of this new representation, news articles data were collected from Reuters and Bloomberg, in addition to the daily close prices of S&P index.

Two different models were built to test the representation: a linear SVM model which have news document as input and +1 or -1 as output indicating increase or decrease in the price for different time frames (1 day, 1 week and 1 month). A non-linear Deep neural network model is also implemented to learn hidden relations between events.

Input features for both linear and nonlinear models were the same: bag-of-words features which use the trivial TFIDF representation after removing stop words and event features represented by different combination of the tuple $(o_1, P, o_2, o_1 + P, P + o_2, o_1 + P + o_2)$ where o_1 is the first object to the left of extracted sentence above and o_2 is the nearest object to the right, and P represents the verb. This feature representation is used to reduce the sparseness of the representation in addition to verb classes.

To evaluate the models, different scenarios were applied. When comparing the results of the models with the bag-of-words articles representation, structured events showed a better performance. From another perspective, when comparing the models, DNN performed better than SVM due to its ability to learn hidden relationships. Moreover, it was distinguished from different timeframes used (1 day, 1 week, 1 month); the shorter the frame the better the results. Thus, the best model was DNN with structured event features for daily prediction with accuracy around 60%.

As shown from the above recent studies based on machine learning, stock price movement can be predicted with an accuracy more than 50% which opposed the EMH and Random walk theory using different timeframes, features, and models. In the next section, we detail our proposed prediction models and highlight its improved performance over the existing models.

3 Proposed Method

The proposed approach is divided into multiple steps, each detailed in this section as follows: Section 3.1 describes the information sources that we have used to build our system. Section 3.2 presents the processing of the data sources. Section 3.3 presents the way news and prices were aligned. Section 3.4 presents the input features. Section 3.5 shows the way data was normalized, and section 3.6 discusses the proposed models.

3.1 Data Sources

Two sources of information are needed for our study: (1) news sentiments and (2) historical prices. Ten years tick data and news data were collected from Reuters platform from January-01-2008 to December 31-2017 for five different stocks AAPL for shared of apple company, GOOGL for google shares, AMZN for amazon shares, FB for Facebook shares. Hence, a tick is a measure of the minimum upward or downward movement in the price. In many cases, a one second timeframe includes many ticks reaching 20 to 30 ticks.

Tick data was collected to include the following details: open bid, close bid, high bid, and low bid, in addition to the time stamp. This high frequency data is collected to do intra-day short-term prediction. Our model requires at least one tick to be released every 1 hour, since we group our data hourly. This huge data requires some preprocessing that takes into consideration the big volume of data (7 trading hours * 3600 = 25200 tick price per day) and the difference in interval between tick data. Tick data might have multiple prices released at the same second and miss some ticks at other seconds. In addition to tick data, we have collected news sentiments. News data includes the stock symbol, date and time issued, source, news headline, sentiment (0 for neutral news, 1 for positive news and -1 for negative news), polarity of negative sentiment, polarity of positive sentiment and polarity of neutral sentiment. The polarity of news is based on the count of positive/negative words in the news article.

3.2 Data Preprocessing

Due to the huge amount of Tick data and to ease the manipulation of data, we have imported our data to MySQL database where sorting data is done when querying.

The initial step was to replace missing ticks. Tick data have different time intervals in the data collected between ticks. This is due to data not being recorded over some time. For example, a second might have four prices recorded and other seconds might not have even one price recorded. To fill missing ticks, we look for the nearest tick data to fill our missing seconds. After importing data to our database and fill missing ticks, we group our data into one-minute time interval where we get the last tick received for each minute recorded in our data. Then, we store clean one-minute data in a new table (no weekends, no ticks outside market open time).

3.3 Aligning news with tick data

Unlike other approaches that filter news outside trading hours and news released during the same interval, we built different scenarios to handle these cases. When generating our data, we give the user an option to choose between one of the following three news scenarios:

1. Last sentiment received on that day based on time to be used: for example, if we want to get the sentiment for 01-03-2010 at 14:00 we, get the last sentiment received on 01-03-2010 before 14:00 and adopt it. If no sentiments exist, we consider the sentiment as neutral.

2. Last sentiment during selected interval of time: if we are grouping our data into hourly time frame, we check the last sentiment released during this hour and consider it as dominant sentiment and if no news released, we consider the sentiment is neutral.

3. Overall average for the day during selected interval: if more than one sentiment is released during the time frame, we calculate the average for positive (a_p), negative (a_n) and neutral (a_{nu}) news (i.e: $a_p = sum(positive\ news)\big/count(all\ news)$ In case of equal sentiments, we sum the polarity of sentiments (polarity of positive sentiment, polarity of negative sentiment, polarity of neutral sentiment features) and check which of these features have the highest summation and consider it the dominant sentiment. In case of equal polarity, we consider neutral sentiment. In this scenario we apply the above formulas on weekend data for Monday sentiment label.

As for the tick data, data features were generated from our one-minute and tick database tables based on hour interval. As such, the input to the machine learning algorithm will be hour data features with one sentiment feature based on one of the above scenarios and the output of the trained model will be the close price of the day.

3.4   Features Generation

Different window sizes have been tested in our models, i.e. how many hours you want to go back when you want to train the models. This will generate our input data in the following format (window size * features).

The features used in our models are as follows:

- Maximum: Maximum price received during the selected hour
- Minimum: Minimum price received during the selected hour
- Average: Average price received during the selected hour
- Standard Deviation: Standard deviation of prices received during the selected hour

$$\sqrt{\frac{1}{N}\sum_{i=1}^{N}(x_i - \frac{\sum p_i}{count(p_i)})^2}$$

- Pseudo Log Return: logarithmic difference between average prices of two consecutive hours.

$$\ln\left(\frac{p_t}{p_{t-1}}\right)$$

where p_t is the average price at time t

- Trend indicator: slope of linear model applied on tick data of the respective hour, which gives an idea about the trend during the last hour.
- Price: Last tick received at selected hour
- Sentiment: News sentiment analysis calculated based on chosen scenario illustrated in section 3.3.

Hence, our input data have 8 features, the formula of number of features is the following:

```
Features=8n where n is window size
```
The output of our model is end of day price.

3.5   Data Normalization

Since the features extracted from the input data are of different units and scale, normalization is needed to scale the data between 0 and 1, which will also help in faster convergence. To normalize our data, we use the *minmaxscaler* function provided by scikit-learn framework. This function gets the max and the min values of each column and performs the following formula:

$$\frac{x_i - \min(x)}{\max(x) - \min(x)}$$

Next, we experiment with various models, namely: Recurrent neural network, Deep neural Network, Support vector Machine and Support vector Regression.

3.6   Models

In this section, we trained different models and compared the effectiveness of recurrent neural network (RNN), feed forward neural network (FFNN), support vector machines (SVM) and support vector regression (SVR) in predicting the direction of today close price with respect to yesterday close price based on the features presented in section 3.4. We tested with the following stocks: AAPL, GOOGL, AMZN and FB for the data collected over 10 years.

For each model, we tried different combinations of window sizes and sentiment scenarios. Window size is a variable, which decides the different number of trading hours during the day; to train our model, we generate data for day d based on first `{4,5,6}` trading hours of the day. The data was normalized and split into two sets: training data of 90% and testing data of 10% for RNN, SVM and SVR models. However, for FFNN we applied the same structure presented in (Arévalo, A. et al. 2016) without data normalization and two data sets: training of 85% and testing of 15%.

FFNN is widely used nowadays for different problems such as classification, regression and pattern recognition in various industries such as financial operations, trading business, analytics and product maintenance. In (Arévalo, A. et al. 2016), the network was formed of 5 layers each with I, 4I/5, 3I/5, 2I/5, I/5 and 1 neuron where I represent the number of inputs. `Tanh` was the activation function used for all hidden layers and linear function for output layer. This network was applied on H2O platform (Arora, A., et al. 2015); a leading open source data science platform. This platform includes the implementation of deep learning algorithms. After splitting the data into 85% training and 15% testing, we trained the model for 50 epochs and applied ADADELTA (Zeiler, M.D 2012) optimization algorithm to improve learning rate learning process. ADADELTA is a per-dimension adaptive learning rate method for gradient descent, where it is not necessary to search parameters for gradient descent manually and is robust to large gradients and noise.

RNN is used for sequence data and differs from DNN by its ability to keep data from previous steps. The memory of RNN could be represented by different cell types: Vanilla RNN (for short term memory), LSTM and GRU (enhance short-term memory of Vanilla RNN using gates mechanism).

In our RNN model, we have tried different network structures with different number of neurons at each layer. We tried different network structure through varying the number of layers between 3 and 7 while varying the number of neurons at each layer between 250 and 5 neurons. We tested the implemented networks to get the best results for -layers and 4-layers networks.

We have trained and tested this model on training and testing datasets generated after normalization. The output is the actual price at end of day. Moreover, we have tried different RNN cells provided by TensorFlow. We trained our model on Basic RNN cell, LSTM cell and GRU cell. We trained the model for 100 epochs and applied ADAMOptimizer as our optimization algorithm to get the best learning rate for our model.

SVM, a supervised machine learning algorithm, can be used for both regression and classification problems. This algorithm uses a kernel trick technique that transforms the data and then finds the optimal boundary between outputs. Moreover, SVM shows that it can perform well on non-linear dataset problems, based on the kernel we choose in training SVM model. SVM have been widely used for stock market prediction. In our SVM model, we have tried different kernel algorithms tuning parameters for each model: Linear, Polynomial and RBF. We have trained and tested this model on our training and testing datasets generated. The output is the binary value, 0 when yesterday close price goes down with respect to today close price and 1 when the price goes up. We used scikit-learn library to build this model and we have trained the model and applied GridSearchCV to choose the best parameters to fit our model.

SVR is the same as SVM, however it is used for regression instead of classification. It uses same terms and functionalities as SVM to predict continuous value. In this model, we follow the same process of SVM except for the output, which is not a class, rather end-of-day price.

4   Results and Discussion

In this section, we show the results obtained for the models defined in section 3.6 on the various stocks. The evaluation metrics are (1) directional accuracy, which analyzes the direction of the predicted value with respect to yesterday close price, (2) Precision, which measures the relevancy of the result, (3) Recall, which measures how many true relevant results returned, and (4) F-measure, which measures the weighted average of precision and recall. Based on the directional accuracy metric (table 2), SVM outperforms RNN, SVR and DNN for different tested stocks. In table 1. We describe the input data.

Table 1. Stock Data Details

Stock Name	Total Data points	Total Articles	output direction
AAPL	19,243	78,036	1,478 positives 1,271 negatives
FB	11,515	30,198	886 positives 759 negatives
GOOGL	8,225	19,829	625 positives 550 negatives
AMZN	19,243	37,265	1,450 positives 1,299 negatives

Table 2. SVM Directional Accuracy Results

Sentiment-Window	Directional Accuracy			
	AAPL	GOOGL	AMZN	FB
S1-4	78.18%	70.94%	75.27%	68.9%
S1-5	83.36%	80.34%	74.91%	73.17%
S1-6	81.73%	79.62%	65.82%	74.66%
S2-4	79.27%	70.94%	74.18%	73.17%
S2-5	82.64%	77.78%	74.18%	74.01%
S2-6	81.09%	79.76%	68.36%	73.27%
S3-4	79.27%	70.09%	75.64%	75%
S3-5	82.91%	76.92%	70.18%	73.78%
S3-6	81.64%	76.62%	68.73%	60.74%

According to Table 2, it is very clear that our SVM model is able to achieve accuracies way above the 50%. When looking at Table 3, it also clear that SVM outperforms SVR, DNN, and RNN. All achieved accuracies are above 75% and in the case of APPL, the achieved accuracy is around 83%. All our models achieved better results than those reported in literature as indicated in Table 4.

Based on the reported results, we summarize our contributions as follows:

- We highlighted the effect of news sentiments on the stock price movement
- We identified best time interval for stock price prediction.
- We identified best news scenario and that each stock is affected differently by news.
- Our model analysis indicates that close price or trend with respect to yesterday close price can be predicted using various AI models.
- Our proposed model can be used in different ways. Firstly, our model can be used by traders without programing information. These traders can use our model either to only predict the variation in price and help traders in their analysis. Also they can use our automated trading system without any monitoring, where the system opens and closes trades based on the predictions. Finally, our code can be easily deployed to do short-term trading.

Table 3. All Models Directional Accuracy

	SVM	SVR	DNN	RNN
APPL	82.91%	79.2%	81.32%	81.3%
AMZN	75.27%	72.26%	74.03%	74.56%
GOOGL	80.34%	66.38%	80.1%	68.38%
FB	75%	68.71%	72.68%	72.39%

Table 4. Related Work Accuracies

Paper	Metric	Value
Arévalo, A. et al. (2016)	Directional Accuracy	66%
Schumaker, R. P. et al. (2009)	Directional Accuracy	71.18%
Ding, X. et al. (2014)	Accuracy	60%

5 Conclusion and Future Work

In this paper, we developed a stock price trend prediction system. To build these models we have gathered data from two sources (i) Historical stock market data from Reuters and (ii) news sentiment released on a certain stock; this data was collected for 4 different stocks over 10 years. Technical features have been calculated and used as input data for our model in addition to 3 scenarios considered when adding sentiments to the calculated features. Our AI framework mainly incorporate DNN, RNN, SVR and SVM for prediction. We tested our proposed prediction model on APPL, AMZN, GOOGL and FB stock shares, for the data collected from (January 1, 2008 to December 31,2017), resulting in a 82.91% accuracy. According to our knowledge, this is the best accuracy achieved in literature so far.

After developing our model, and to show its performance we would implement a risk strategy to check the profits we would gain based on our predictions and a few enhancements can be done and studied for our prediction model. One direction is to add extra technical indicators used in stock market. Another direction would be trying different time-frames for grouping our data. Finally, we could try to enhance the prediction of the exact price.

References

Weng, B., Ahmed, M. A., & Megahed, F. M. (2017). Stock market one-day ahead movement prediction using disparate data sources. Expert Systems with Applications,79, 153-163. doi:10.1016/j.eswa.2017.02.041

Li, X., Huang, X., Deng, X., & Zhu, S. (2014). Enhancing quantitative intra-day stock return prediction by integrating both market news and stock prices information. Neurocomputing, 142, 228-238. doi:10.1016/j.neucom.2014.04.043

Arévalo, A., Niño, J., Hernández, G., & Sandoval, J. (2016). High-Frequency Trading Strategy Based on Deep Neural Networks. Intelligent Computing Methodologies Lecture Notes in Computer Science, 424436. doi:10.1007/978-3-319-42297-8_40

Horne, J. C., & Parker, G. G. (1967). The Random-Walk Theory: An Empirical Test. Financial Analysts Journal, 23(6), 87-92. doi:10.2469/faj.v23.n6.87

Fama, E. F. (1970). Efficient Capital Markets: A Review of Theory and Empirical Work. The Journal of Finance, 25(2), 383. doi:10.2307/2325486

Schumaker, R. P., & Chen, H. (2009). A quantitative stock prediction system based on financial news. Information Processing & Management, 45(5), 571-583. doi:10.1016/j.ipm.2009.05.001

Ding, X., Zhang, Y., Liu, T., & Duan, J. (2014). Using Structured Events to Predict Stock Price Movement: An Empirical Investigation. Proceedings of the

2014 Conference on Empirical Methods in Natural Language Processing (EMNLP). doi:10.3115/v1/d14-1148

Schumaker, R. P., & Chen, H. (2009). A quantitative stock prediction system based on financial news. Information Processing & Management, 45(5), 571-583. doi:10.1016/j.ipm.2009.05.001

Bollen, J., & Mao, H. (2011). Twitter Mood as a Stock Market Predictor. Computer,44(10), 91-94. doi:10.1109/mc.2011.323

Arora, A., et al.: Deep Learning with H2O (2015)

learning process 20. Zeiler, M.D.: ADADELTA: An Adaptive Learning Rate Method, 6 (2012)

learning process 20. Zeiler, M.D.: ADADELTA: An Adaptive Learning Rate Method, 6 (2012)

Investopedia. "World's Greatest Investors." Investopedia, Investopedia, 9 July 2008, www.investopedia.com/slide-show/worlds-greatest-investors/.

Singh, Aishwarya. "Predicting the Stock Market Using Machine Learning and Deep Learning." Analytics Vidhya, 26 July 2019, www.analyticsvidhya.com/blog/2018/10/predicting-stock-price-machine-learningnd-deep-learning-techniques-python/.

Mark L. Mitchell and J. Harold Mulherin The Journal of Finance Vol. 49, No. 3, Papers and Proceedings Fifty-Fourth Annual Meeting of the American Finance Association, Boston, Massachusetts, January 3-5, 1994 (Jul., 1994), pp. 923-950

Active Learning for Financial Investment Reports

Sian Gooding and Ted Briscoe
Dept of Computer Science and Technology
University of Cambridge
{shg36|ejb}@cam.ac.uk

Abstract

Investment reports contain qualitative information from numerous sources. Due to the huge volume of online business information, it is increasingly difficult for financial analysts to track and read all relevant texts. In this paper, we develop a novel tool to assist financial analysts when writing an investment report. We perform multi-class classification on business texts to categorise them into informative investment topics. Using active learning we show that we can obtain the same F1-score of 0.74 with 58% less data.

1 Introduction

Financial analysts guide investors and asset managers in their investment choices (Knorr Cetina and Preda, 2012) by providing investment research information, recommendations, advice or market decisions (Bauman and Dowen, 1988). Such information is typically presented in report format and used by investors to inform portfolio decisions (Baker and Haslem, 1973).

Investment reports contain information from numerous sources and aim to present facts in a coherent and readily intelligible manner (Graham et al., 1934). As well as quantitative measures, investment reports cover a wide range of qualitative topics such as customer satisfaction, brand recognition, and corporate social responsibility (Huang et al., 2014).

Due to the rise of online resources, the availability and accessibility of business information has rapidly increased (Fogarty and Rogers, 2005). Owing to this, it is often infeasible for a financial analyst to keep track of, let alone read, all available information on a given company (Seo et al., 2004).

In this paper we present an automated pipeline to identify and categorise pertinent investment in-formation. We incorporate our models into an active learning framework, allowing financial analysts to train the system with a minimal number of annotated examples. We envision our system being used to assist financial analysts in acquiring and categorising relevant company information.

2 Background

2.1 Financial Text Mining

Prior work on textual classification in the investment domain has extensively focused on the prediction of financial markets (Nassirtoussi et al., 2014). More specifically, algorithms are trained to predict stock price movements using text information from a range of online sources, e.g., the Financial Times, Reuters, or the Wall Street Journal (Cho et al., 1999).

A review by Mittermayer and Knolmayer (2006) compares eight text mining prototypes used for predicting short-term market trends. All prototypes rely exclusively on text-based features. The systems opted for either expertly hand-crafted features or features automatically inferred by models. Most of the financial performances obtained by the systems are moderate; Mittermayer and Knolmayer (2006) argue that this is due, in part, to the systems not considering quantitative information. However, they acknowledge that qualitative information is highly informative. For example, when a company reports that it received a 'takeover bid' the crucial data is not in a numerical format.

A further application of financial text mining, similar to the production of investment reports, is that of automated portfolio management. Portfolio management involves the monitoring of current investments by finding, filtering and evaluating relevant information. Warren is a multi-agent system for intelligent portfolio management by Seo et al. (2004). This system enables users to keep track of both quantitative (e.g., stock price, performance history) and qualitative information in the form of online financial news reports. The text mining component of Warren, referred to as TextMiner (Seo et al., 2002), performs text classification on financial articles. TextMiner uses a combination of word feature sets and a variant of the weighted majority algorithm to classify news articles. Articles are classified into one of five classes, each class aims to represent the financial performance of the company based on the article, for instance *good, good-uncertain, neutral*. TextMiner achieves a 75% average accuracy across all classes. One difficulty the authors note is that the system struggles when presented with phrases from multiple classes, for example 'Company B shares rose 5% contrasting with A where shares fell by 7%'. Warren uses sets of words as features e.g., 'shares rose','shares fell', but is unable to link these to relevant entities.

Unlike the previous systems presented in Mittermayer and Knolmayer (2006), we do not aim to predict the impact of relevant business information directly on stock prices. Neither do we attempt to classify text according to the financial impact like the Warren system. Instead, our system is designed to present useful and targeted information from a financial analyst's perspective. To the best of our knowledge this is the first system designed for this task.

2.2 Active Learning

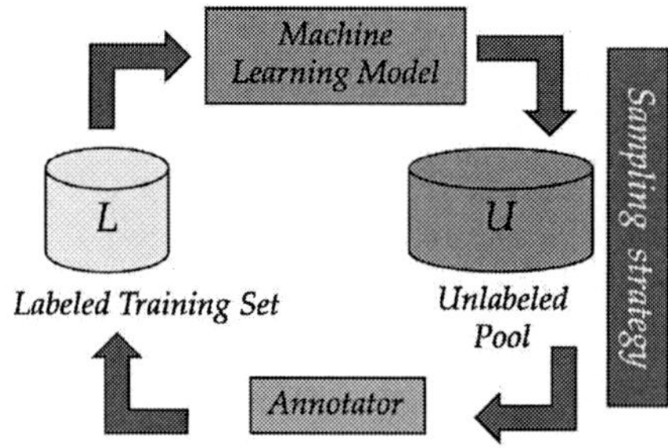

Figure 1: Active learning cycle

Annotated data is hard and expensive to obtain, notably in specialised domains where only experts can provide reliable labels (Konyushkova et al., 2017). Active learning allows machine learning classifiers to achieve higher accuracies with fewer training instances by enabling the classifier to interactively query data points. Active learning is well-motivated in many modern machine learning problems where data may be abundant but labels are scarce or expensive to acquire (Settles, 2009).

Figure 1 shows a classic active learning scenario; whereby a machine learning model has access to an unlabelled pool of data and an *uncertainty sampling strategy* is used to select the most informative instances for labelling. Once the most informative instances have been labelled they are added to the training set and the model is then retrained.

Our motivation for incorporating an active learning framework into the system is two-fold:

1. **Annotator Resource**
   Gathering labelled data for this task is time-consuming and requires the expertise of experienced financial analysts. Maximising the utility of the labelled data allows for better models with fewer labelled instances, saving valuable resources.

2. **Category Introduction**
   When writing financial reports the relevant qualitative categories are subject to change over time. Since new labels may be introduced by financial analysts it is important that the model is able to prioritise acquiring labels for new topics.

3 Data

The data set used in this project was collected by All Street Research[1] ("All Street"), who specialise in creating intelligent tools for financial analysis. It was created using online business resources annotated by financial analysts. Analysts were asked to select information that they would consider useful when writing an investment report. This selected text was then labelled according to the category of the investment report it was relevant to. An example of annotated text from the data set is shown in Table 1.

The total data set collected contained 3097 instances, with individual categories defined by analysts. However, several categories contained less than 100 examples which meant they were not large enough to train and test our framework. We therefore limit the data set to topics that have at least 100 instances. The resulting data set consists of 1824 examples and 11 categories; a breakdown of the categories is shown in Table 2. The category

---

[1]https://www.allstreet.org

HOSuN fuses our global physical supply chain with a global information supply chain, enabling complete visibility into the status of products at all times. This makes our management of the supply process more efficient. Through HOSuN, we can also use predictive analytics to anticipate future demand patterns. This knowledge is crucial for the efficient production and cost reduction of biologic and vaccine products.

Artificial Intelligence　　Cost Reduction　　Supply Chain　　Not Labelled

Table 1: Example of analyst annotated text

with most examples (340) was *Artificial Intelligence*, with samples of text covering many areas such as 'data mining', 'machine learning' and 'big data'. The smallest category was *Wellbeing* consisting of 196 examples. The mean word length across examples in each topic is reported; the category *Human Capital* had the highest average word count (575) and *Culture* the lowest (380).

Category	Total	Mean Length
Artificial Intelligence	340	430
Business Process Innovation	137	426
Climate Action	228	557
Cost Reduction	120	416
Culture	106	380
Customer Service	160	555
Enterprise Solutions	129	425
Human Capital	119	575
Quality Education	109	532
Supply Chain Management	180	393
Wellbeing	196	476

Table 2: Data set categories alongside the total number of examples and the mean word length

4 Method

Our classification pipeline consists of three steps, which are embedded into an active learning framework. The classification pipeline is outlined in Section 4.1, and the active learning settings are described in Section 4.2.

4.1 Topic Classification Pipeline

4.1.1 Preprocessing

The first stage of classification involves preprocessing the text. In the samples provided we initially remove any corporate named entities, names of people and stop words using spaCy.[2] In the wild, our system is provided with the URLs of relevant web pages; text is then scraped from the page and the pre-processing is performed on paragraph content. Irrelevant content such as page headings are disregarded at this stage.

4.1.2 Feature Selection

Our system relies on word features as it aims to identify terms or bigrams that are highly indicative of a given class. We use functions from the scikit-learn[3] library to transform the total vocabulary of our training set to a matrix of token counts. We then apply a scikit-learn transformer in order to produce a normalized *tf-idf* representation of content. This technique is a common term weighting scheme used in information retrieval and document classification. The goal of using *tf-idf* instead of raw word frequencies is to minimise the impact of highly frequent tokens across a corpus, thereby maximising the importance of class-discriminative terms. Using this technique we are able to investigate which terms are most discriminative for a given class. Examples of the most informative terms for the *Artificial Intelligence* and *Climate Action* classes are shown in Figure 2.

4.1.3 Model Selection

We tested a range of multi-class models using stratified 5-fold cross-validation. The average macro F1-score across all classes is reported for the top three performing classifiers in Table 3.

Classifier	F1-score
Linear SVC (calibrated)	0.74
Linear SVC	0.72
Logistic Regression	0.71
Random Forest	0.69

Table 3: Results

The best performance on this data set was by the linear support vector (SVC) model. Cali-

---

[2]https://github.com/explosion/spaCy

[3]https://scikit-learn.org

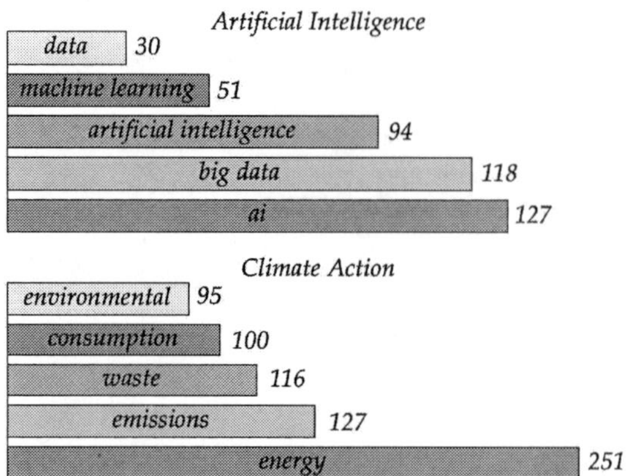

Figure 2: Terms with highest *tf-idf* value for the classes *Artificial Intelligence* and *Climate Action*, shown with class occurrence counts

brated SVC results are obtained using a cross-validation estimator which enables automatic hyper-parameter selection using cross-validation on the training set. The best parameter settings across 5 folds are averaged for prediction on the test set. A more in-depth analysis of classifier results is presented in Section 5.

4.2 Active Learning

As outlined in Section 2.2, uncertainty based active learning requires an *uncertainty sampling strategy* (Lewis and Gale, 1994). This strategy allows an active learner to query the instances that it is least certain about labelling (Settles, 2009). We use three uncertainty sampling strategies, described below, and compare their effectiveness. In the following, x^* denotes the most informative instance from an unlabelled set. To illustrate the sampling strategies we reference a three class example with two data points, shown in Table 4.

Data	Class 1	Class 2	Class 3
1	0.60	0.40	0.00
2	0.50	0.25	0.25

Table 4: Example multi-class probability distribution for two data points

4.2.1 Least Confidence Sampling

This technique considers which of the unlabelled instances has the lowest maximum confidence (Lewis and Gale, 1994):

$$x^*_{LC} = \underset{x}{\mathrm{argmax}}\, 1 - P_\theta(\hat{y}|x),$$

where $\hat{y} = \mathrm{argmax}_x\, P_\theta(y|x)$, or the class label with the highest posterior probability under the model θ.

For instance, of the two data points in Table 4 the highest probability across classes is 0.60 and 0.50 for 1 and 2 respectively. Data point 2 has the lowest maximum confidence and therefore the active learner would request this label.

4.2.2 Margin Sampling

Multi-class margin sampling (Scheffer et al., 2001) considers the two highest class probabilities $\hat{y}_1$ and $\hat{y}_2$:

$$x^*_M = \underset{x}{\mathrm{argmin}}\, P_\theta(\hat{y}_1|x) - P_\theta(\hat{y}_2|x),$$

If there is a large margin between $\hat{y}_1$ and $\hat{y}_2$ then the model is able to discriminate clearly. However, if there is a close margin the model is unsure which class to choose making x a good candidate for labelling.

In our example, the highest two probabilities for point 1 and 2 are $0.60, 0.40$ and $0.50, 0.25$. The difference between these is lower for point 1, therefore the label for this instance should be queried.

4.2.3 Entropy Sampling

The final sampling technique considered uses *entropy* (Shannon, 1948) as an uncertainty measure:

$$x^*_H = \underset{x}{\mathrm{argmax}} - \sum_i P_\theta(y_i|x) \log P_\theta(y_i|x),$$

where y_i ranges over all possible labels. *Entropy* is an information-theoretic measure that numerically represents the amount of information needed to "encode" a distribution. Entropy is commonly used as an indication of uncertainty or impurity in machine learning (Settles, 2009). For the example in Table 4, the entropy value for point 1 is 0.67 whilst the value for 2 is 1.04. Therefore, point 2 having the highest entropy value would be chosen for labelling.

5 Results

5.1 Active Learning Results

In this section we present the results for each *uncertainty sampling strategy*. To compare the impact of intelligently selecting data for labelling, these techniques are presented alongside a random baseline. The baseline represents the average performance across 5 runs with random data

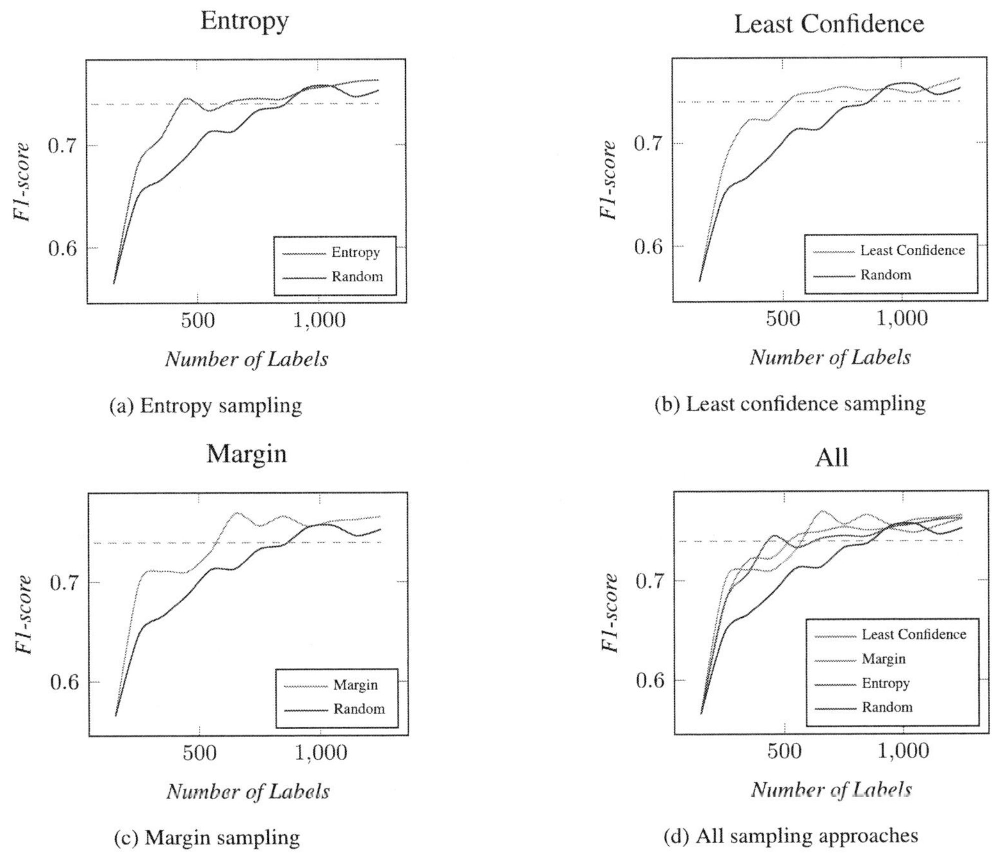

(a) Entropy sampling   (b) Least confidence sampling

(c) Margin sampling   (d) All sampling approaches

Figure 3: Active learning results

sampling. The classification model used in all settings is the *calibrated SVC*, as this was the best performing model shown in Section 4.1.3. In order to test how effective the active learning techniques would be in practice, we simulate annotation by withholding labels from our current data set and provide them when the active learner queries for the label. The number of labels provided is shown along the x axis. The initial model is trained with 150 random labelled instances; the model is then retrained with additional labels requested by the uncertainty sampling strategy. Once retrained, the F1-score is calculated using a held-out test set of size 548.

Entropy, as shown in Figure 3a, is a highly successful uncertainty sampling approach. The dashed line marks an F1-score of 0.74, as this was the best score achieved with 5-fold cross-validation on the total data set. Using entropy sampling the model is able to achieve an F1-score of 0.74 with only 448 labelled examples. As the initial model is trained with a random 150 instances, only 298 labels are requested by the clas-

sifier to reach this score. In comparison, the random baseline requires 710 additional data points. This means our active learner can achieve the same score with 42% of the labelled data needed by a non-active classifier.

Least confidence sampling, illustrated in Figure 3b, achieves an F1-score of 0.74 with only 313 additional labels. As for entropy-based sampling, the initial improvement gradient is steep. Within the first 200 additional labels, the model improvement using least confidence sampling is 0.18, which is double the improvement of the baseline 0.09.

As shown in Figure 3c, margin sampling achieves an F1-score of 0.74 with 382 additional labels, the most labels required of all active techniques for this score. However, the initial improvement gradient is the highest of all sampling strategies. Furthermore, margin sampling reaches an impressive F1-score of 0.77 with 486 labelled items, surpassing the results of all other techniques and the baseline.

Figure 3d shows all three uncertainty sampling approaches and the random baseline. The sam-

Category	Precision	Recall	F1-score
Artificial Intelligence (104)	0.79	0.84	0.81
Business Innovation (41)	0.62	0.53	0.57
Climate Action (70)	0.96	0.93	0.94
Cost Reduction (35)	0.70	0.74	0.72
Culture (26)	0.72	0.69	0.71
Customer Service (51)	0.90	0.88	0.89
Enterprise Solutions (38)	0.62	0.53	0.57
Human Capital (35)	0.81	0.86	0.83
Quality Education (28)	0.77	0.86	0.81
Supply Chain (58)	0.73	0.79	0.76
Wellbeing (62)	0.88	0.79	0.83

Table 5: Precision, recall and weighted F1-score across classes in the test set

pling strategy that reached an F1-score of 0.74 first was entropy-based, followed by least confidence and then margin. All techniques exhibit a degree of variance during retraining, resulting in performance peaks and troughs. To counteract this, our framework monitors performance and saves the best performing models.

5.2 Model Results

The highest F1-score of 0.77 is achieved using margin uncertainty sampling with 747 labelled instances. Comparatively, the highest baseline score is 0.76 and requires 1216 labelled instances. The reason the random baseline does not achieve an F1-score of 0.77, even when trained with the total data set, may be due to the fact that the calibrated SVC re-tunes optimal parameters at each training step. Therefore, parameters for all models will depend on the order of labels they were presented with.

Table 5 presents the performance across classes for this model. A confusion matrix is provided in Appendix A.1. The best performance is achieved on the *climate action* class where 65 of the 70 instances in the test set are labelled correctly. The worst performance is on *Business Innovation* and *Enterprise Solutions*, both with a weighted F1-score of 0.57. A closer inspection of the misclassifications for these classes provides an insight into why performance declines. For instance, consider example (1):

(1) We fuse our global supply chain with an information supply chain, enabling complete visibility into the status of products at all times. In turn making our management of the supply process more efficient.

This has been attributed the label *enterprise solution* and is misclassified into the *supply chain* cate-

gory. This raises the question of whether segments of text could be attributed multiple labels in future labelling scenarios if they are relevant to multiple classes.

6 Conclusion

To conclude, we have built a classification pipeline that can be used with online business resources to categorise investment-related content. The pipeline is incorporated into an active learning framework, allowing financial analysts to train effective models with as few as 448 labelled examples. Our best performing active learning model achieves an F1-score of 0.77 with 747 instances. In practice there would be a much larger unlabelled data set, allowing the model more variety and choice when requesting data to be labelled.

In future work we aim to integrate additional features into our topic classification pipeline, as well as test our active learning loop in the wild with financial analysts. Further to this, we recognise a drawback of our current approach is that we do not initially filter for content relevancy. Therefore we plan to investigate techniques of disregarding repeated or irrelevant information prior to multi-class classification.

Acknowledgements

We would like to thank All Street[4] and Innovate UK[5] for funding this project and providing the data.

---

[4] https://www.allstreet.org
[5] https://www.gov.uk/government/organisations/innovate-uk/about

References

H Kent Baker and John A Haslem. 1973. Information needs of individual investors. *Journal of accountancy*, pages 64–69.

W Scott Bauman and Richard Dowen. 1988. Growth projections and commin stock returns. *Financial Analysts Journal*, 44(4):79.

V Cho, B Wüthrich, and J Zhang. 1999. Text processing for classification. *Journal of Computational Intelligence in Finance*, 7(2):6–22.

Timothy J Fogarty and Rodney K Rogers. 2005. Financial analysts' reports: an extended institutional theory evaluation. *Accounting, Organizations and Society*, 30(4):331–356.

Benjamin Graham, David Le Fevre Dodd, Sidney Cottle, et al. 1934. *Security analysis*. McGraw-Hill New York.

Allen H Huang, Amy Y Zang, and Rong Zheng. 2014. Evidence on the information content of text in analyst reports. *The Accounting Review*, 89(6):2151–2180.

Karin Knorr Cetina and Alex Preda. 2012. *The Oxford handbook of the sociology of finance*. Oxford University Press.

Ksenia Konyushkova, Raphael Sznitman, and Pascal Fua. 2017. Learning active learning from data. In *Advances in Neural Information Processing Systems*, pages 4225–4235.

David D Lewis and William A Gale. 1994. A sequential algorithm for training text classifiers. In *SIGIR94*, pages 3–12. Springer.

Marc-André Mittermayer and Gerhard Knolmayer. 2006. *Text mining systems for market response to news: A survey*. Institut für Wirtschaftsinformatik der Universität Bern.

Arman Khadjeh Nassirtoussi, Saeed Aghabozorgi, Teh Ying Wah, and David Chek Ling Ngo. 2014. Text mining for market prediction: A systematic review. *Expert Systems with Applications*, 41(16):7653–7670.

Tobias Scheffer, Christian Decomain, and Stefan Wrobel. 2001. Active hidden markov models for information extraction. In *International Symposium on Intelligent Data Analysis*, pages 309–318. Springer.

Young-Woo Seo, Joseph Giampapa, and Katia Sycara. 2002. Text classification for intelligent portfolio management. Technical report, Carnegie-Mellon University Pittsburgh PA Robotics Institute.

Young-Woo Seo, Joseph Giampapa, and Katia Sycara. 2004. Financial news analysis for intelligent portfolio management. Technical report, Carnegie-Mellon University Pittsburgh PA Robotics Institute.

Burr Settles. 2009. Active learning literature survey. Technical report, University of Wisconsin-Madison Department of Computer Sciences.

Claude E Shannon. 1948. A note on the concept of entropy. *Bell System Tech. J*, 27(3):379–423.

A Appendix

A.1 Model Confusion Matrix

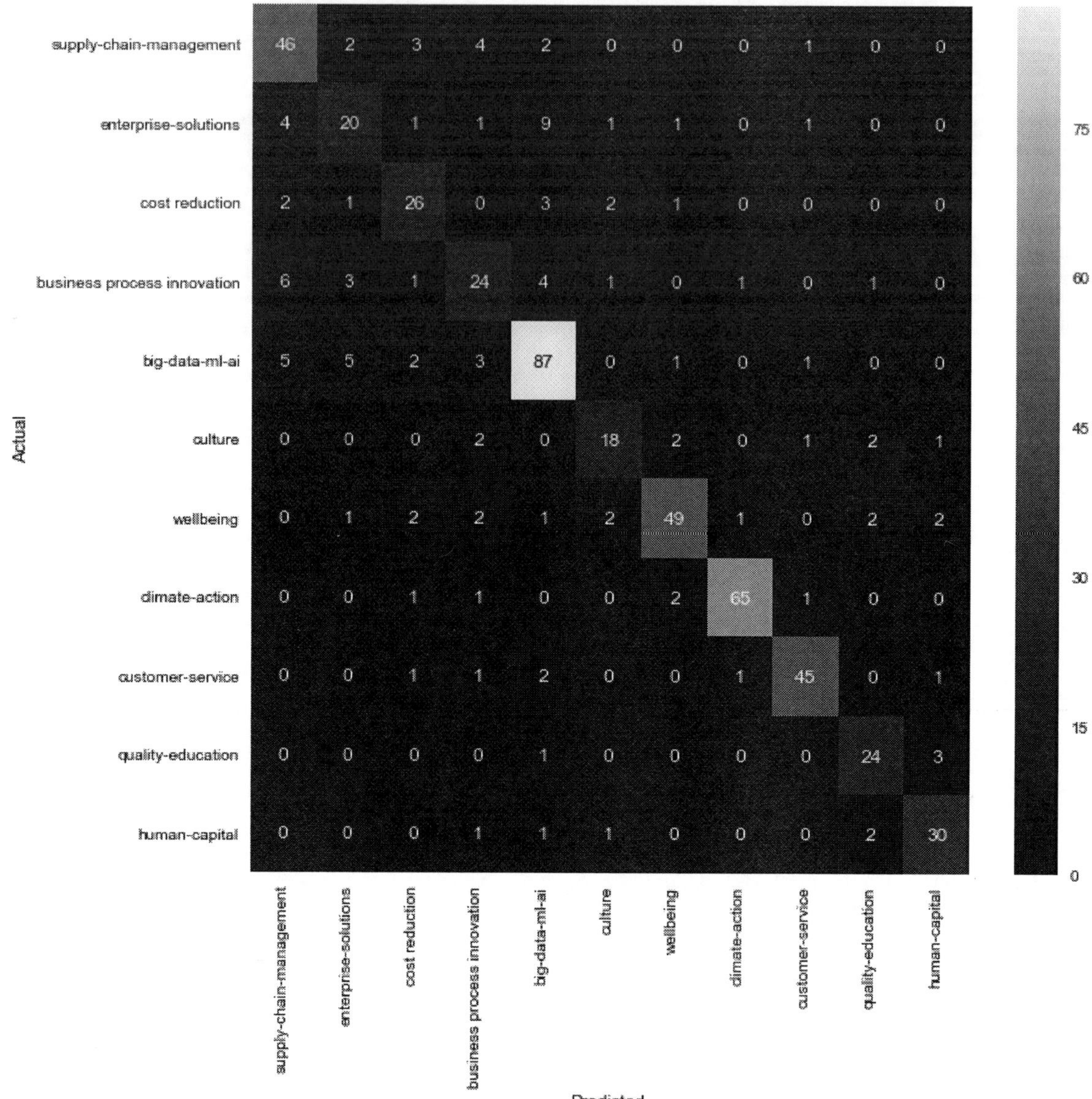

Figure 4: Confusion matrix for best performing margin sampling model

Towards Unlocking the Narrative of the United States Income Tax Forms

Esme Manandise
Intuit Futures
Mountain View, California, USA
esme_manandise@intuit.com

Abstract

The present study contributes to the literature on the language of the tax-and-regulations domain in the context of highly-formatted tax forms published by a federal agency. Content and form analyses rely on a methodology that looks for meaning and patterns in connection to the main purpose of income tax filing, i.e. figuring out calculations to determine whether taxes were overpaid or owed to the United States Internal Revenue Service. Profiling the income-tax forms by spelling out language regularities across the set has at least two advantages. Firstly, profiling contributes to the understanding of how the *2010 Plain Writing Act* mandate of *'clear and simple'* writing is being achieved—if at all. Secondly, profiling a small, unannotated corpus can help determine the Natural Language Processing approach best fitted to extract, represent, and execute automatically tax calculations expressed as arithmetic word problems.

1   Introduction

The term "narratives" refers to accounts of ideas or connected *'events'*, whether factual or not, through oral or written communication. Narrative understanding and qualitative content analysis are related tasks as they study the practices, beliefs, needs, and values of groups of individuals. Other than eliciting universal lamentation—independently of one's moral view on the necessity of taxation for a civil society, the tax-and-regulations domain on the communication dimension is not popular with practitioners of discourse analysis, narrative exploration, or natural language automation. Narratives are stories and, to most, there isn't much storytelling in the tax-and-regulations domain—though a 1040 tax-return form the size of a postcard made a good *yarn*.

In the most literal sense, tax forms consist of embedded *stories* with words, phrases, sentences, fragments and tables through which run threads to output dollar amounts—as input to tax-form lines or as the final amount (refundable to taxpayer or owed to the Internal Revenue Service (IRS)). Tax forms, and their associated schedules and worksheets, provide instructions and clarifications as well as prompt taxpayers for qualitative and quantitative personal information. In addition, distributed throughout a form and across forms, are arithmetic word problems of varying complexity. To solve them, filers must understand content and handle amounts as input

Forms	Segments
F4868	Late filing penalty is usually charged if your return is filed after the due date. The penalty is usually 5% of the amount due for each month or part of a month your return is late. The maximum penalty is 25%. If your return is more than 60 days late, the minimum penalty is $210 (adjusted for inflation) or the balance of the tax due on your return, whichever is smaller
F8829	Line C times line D divided by 12 times $5.00 times line E
F1041	If line 25 is larger than the total of lines 23 and 26, enter amount overpaid.
F2441	Add the amounts on lines 12 and 13 and subtract from that total the amount on line 14.
F8941WKS	If the result is not a multiple of $1,000, round the result down to the next lowest multiple of $1,000
F8949	Add the amounts in columns (d), (e), (g), and (h) (subtract negative amounts)

Table 1: Calculations as Raw Text

to basic operations (addition, subtraction, multiplication, division, percentage conversion, rounding). Sometimes, to complete the calculation, they must make the arithmetic operation explicit. With stacked operations, they must apply the operations in their correct order. Consider the examples in Table 1 above.

Tax forms are published by the IRS which, as a federal government agency, complies with the *Plain Writing Act* of 2010. The language in tax forms is supposedly '*clear and simple*' to help with content understanding. Simplicity should encourage filers to comply[1] with the Tax Law.

For natural language processing (NLP) tasks which consume raw text as input, the mandate '*clear and simple*' is an ideal convenience. Can we discover how '*clear and simple*' is instantiated in tax forms? Has '*clear and simple*' turned the language of tax forms, schedules, and worksheets into an unequivocally-specific language register? Does '*clear and simple*' remove semantic and syntactic ambiguities? One of our goals in referencing the notion of '*clear and simple*' is to gain exploratory insight into the language of tax forms with the ultimate purpose of using raw text as input to the automatic (no human-in-the-loop.) detection and execution of calculations by an NLP system.

In this paper, we describe a preprocessing implementation for detecting and labeling executable calculations in raw text. More specifically, we concentrate on feature-based classifications to build a profile of the United States income-tax forms set as a whole rather than per-document profiles. Ultimately, our investigation may help to assess whether '*clear and simple*' is measurable or merely a matter of opinion[2].

2   Related Work

To the best of our knowledge, there are no publications in English that detail the language and discourse of the income-tax forms in the tax-and-regulations domain. However, glossaries of tax terms are aplenty; they are made available online and/or are published by government agencies[3], private outfits[4] and international organizations[5]; some glossaries are integrated in tax and accounting software[6]. While tax terms are important as they correspond to concepts and entities in the domain, tax-and-regulations texts do not consist merely of a collection of terms. The reductionist view that to learn the tax language is to learn its terms considers the tax language a *Toki Pona*—a pidgin of sort. Terms need to be connected by relations for tax text to be coherent.

Recently, some Tax Law scholars have shown an interest in the language of taxes as it appears in IRS publications. They have focused on the federal government agency mandate to output text in a '*clear and simple*' language. Most noticeably, Blank et al. (2017) discuss instances where the IRS transformed '*complex, often ambiguous tax law into seemingly simple statements*'. Achieving language simplicity can cause a loss of information and make content less accurate. The authors summarize their findings in three categories: (1) '*contested tax law presented through language simplification as clear tax rules*', (2) '*failure to explain the tax law with possible exceptions*', (3) tax law rewording by IRS. They discuss concrete language examples. How the change from the adverb '*materially*' in Treasury regulations to the adverb '*significantly*' in IRS publications can create uncertainty in filers when determining exclusions from taxable income of gain from the sale of a principal residence.

3   Income Tax Form Set

To build the profile, we use 234 IRS tax forms, schedules, and worksheets (individual and fiduciary) for the 2017 tax year. These are published in English in PDF format (see sample in Figure 1.) The forms have a visually-complex structure consisting of a mix of raw text as free-standing paragraphs and of tables with rows and columns, headers, instructions, cautionary notes, line labels, checkboxes, input fields, etc. (see Figure 1 below.)

We use a machine-learning-based algorithm to extract raw text from the PDF-formatted files. The context of raw text (occurrence in original layout) is recorded because the text '*position*', in

---

[1] According to the IRS (Blank et al. (2017)), 56% of filers use third-party advisors, 34% rely on tax preparation software, and 10% of individuals file without assistance.
[2] Tax forms have a readership of around 140,000 million filers with no uniformity in educational background or English-language literacy.

[3] For instance, IRS.gov, efile.com, psu.instructure.com
[4] For instance, law and accounting practitioners (Taxman.com or taxWorld.com)
[5] For instance, Organisation for Economic Co-operation and Development
[6] For instance, TurboTax

particular when occurring in tables, can be relevant to its interpretation.

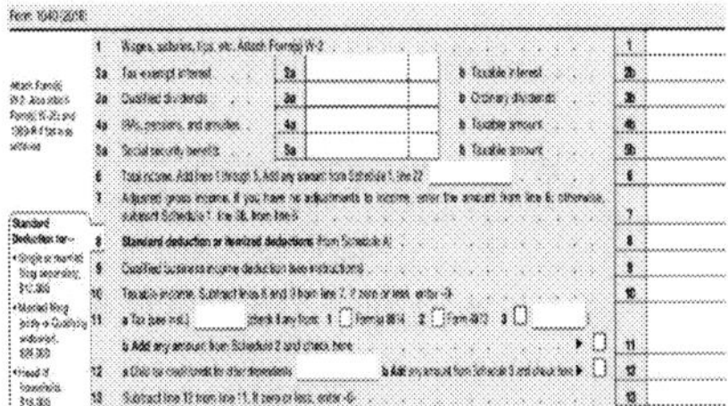

Figure 1: Income Tax Form Sample

4 A Brief Overview of the Nature of the Income Tax Narrative

The underlying schema of an income tax form narrative[7] is that of a camera-eye narration with purely matter-of-fact representation of facts, events, and actions to be taken. The text reads like a transcription with fragmentary content sequentially displayed and/or distributed across columns. The timeline between facts, events, and actions is punctuated with form-name and line references, with spatial and situational pointers like '*above*' or '*this*' as well as with temporal references such as '*current*' or '*past-due*'. Even though the narrative protagonist is referred to in the second person, the pronoun '*you*' means '*anyone*' who is filing an income tax return.

Deixis is present throughout the text of income tax forms. Deixis curates the filer's path to help complete income tax return filing. However, it is up to the filer to assign denotational meaning to deictic expressions.

And then do the maths!

5 Form Set Description and Classifications

To address the problem of the tax-form language and its embedded stories, we use descriptive statistics and classifiers with features that have immediate practical significance for the tax domain.

PDF extraction outputs structured json files wherein named fields hold various types of source data. The field of most immediate interest for our purpose is the field[8] named '*paragraph*'. Before we classify the content, we automatically segment[9] the paragraphs into a collection of individual segments. We do not use the notion of

sentence, which implies the marker '*tense*' (however instantiated in the tax language). Given that content relevant to calculations may be a table header or a text fragment that points to an amount referenced by a line number, we use '*segment*' to refer to the minimal string unit used in the analysis (and as input to the NLP annotation preprocessor.) Currently, to create the tax-form profile, the NLP preprocessor only inspects content and collects information on individual segments.

5.1 A Lexical Paradigm for Feature-based Classifications

Our NLP annotation uses 2 lexical resources: (1) base lexicon for single tokens and (2) term lexicon for multiword expressions (MWE) corresponding to tax concepts and entities. The base lexicon is a repository of granular knowledge about single tokens in the domain. Many words in the base lexicon correspond to the head of a term at the phrase level, i.e. heads of terms are subject to morphological changes such as singular/plural. For instance, the single-token concept '*expense*' is the head of the MWE '*daycare expenses*' or '*research and experimental expenses*'.

Both resources have been populated automatically by mining IRS income-tax forms, schedules, worksheets, publications, and TurboTax interviews. After completion, the base lexicon was vetted by specialists.

add	{ pos:verb, arg1:obj, arg2:prep_to, arg3:prep_on, arg4:prep_through prep_thru, arg5:prep_for, semtype:arithmetic_operation, accumulation tr:arg1toarg2, syn:combine, sum, total, freqs: ......}
total	{ pos:adj, pos:noun, pos:verb, arg1:prep_from, arg2:prep_on, arg3:prep_for, semtype: arithmetic_operation accumulation amount outcome property, tgtwd:sum, syn:add, freqs: ......}

Table 2: Lexical Key-Values Pair Sample

Lexical entries in the lexica have been designed as a pair *{key:values}*. The values themselves can be of the type *{key:values}*. The '*values*' fields have been augmented with Wordnet and in-house-Wordnet-like features to describe granular

---

[7] In its instructions, the IRS uses the notion of narrative to describe the process for filing specific forms like F990 or F13424-M.

[8] Issues with PDF extraction are reflected in paragraph fields as text can be inaccurately split or glommed together.

[9] Segmentation relies on linefeed tags or predefined diacritics such as semi-colon or period.

morphological, semantic, syntactic, and domain-idiosyncratic properties of the keys. Consider the entries '*add*' and '*total*' (listed in Table 2 above in abbreviated format.)

Segments are tokenized; then each token is lemmatized to enable base form matching in the lexica. When matching is successful, the lexical information (*values* field) associated with the keys is retrieved. The built-in classifiers rely on these lexically-specified value features to automatically compute segment classifications as well as flag features that can be problematic to parsing such as scope of coordination or attachment points for prepositional phrases[10]. The preprocessor collates together a shallow description for each segment.

This classification strategy was adopted to generate reports, search and group segments on clusters of shared features (in abbreviated format here):

1	Segment	if more than one form 8611 is filed, add the line 14 amounts from all forms and enter the total on the appropriate line of your return.
	Features	Arith operation_0-MWE_Tensed_Coordination_ Conditional_Posambiguity_PP
2	Segment	enter your 2017 regular income tax liability minus allowable credits (see instructions)
	Features	Arith operation_2-MWE-3w-2w-_Tensed_Verb-like_Parens

Table 3: Segment Feature Labeling Sample

For instance, the feature-aggregate label informs that segment 1 is an arithmetic operation with no MWE as operands and that some conditions need to be met for the operation to apply. As for segment 2, the label classifies it as an arithmetic operation with a verb-like operator *minus*. There are 2 multiword expressions '*income tax liability*' and '*allowable credit*', of 3- and 2-words, respectively; these MWE are operand candidates. In addition, there is parenthetical material that will need checking during parsing.

This labeling schema allows us to readily search the form set as a collection of segments. For instance, there are 3,970 segments labeled '*arithmetic operation*', but only 5.18% of these

use '*minus*', '*plus*', or '*times*' to express subtraction, addition, or multiplication.

5.2 General Descriptive Statistics

The United States income-tax-form set for the 2017 tax year is a small collection of 234 forms. After the PDF extraction of the structured content of tax forms, paragraphs are retrieved and each paragraph is, in turn, broken down into separate

Total Number of (No.)	
Individual forms	234
Paragraphs	15,294
Single segments	41,660
Single words[1]	349,146
Segments with terms	18,164
Unique words	6,424
Unique alphabetic words	4,812
Unique non-alphabetic words	1,612
Average No. single words per sentence	8.46
Average sentence length	15.82
No. terms	23,840

Table 4: General Statistics

Word	Rank	Percent
line	1	04.90%
the	2	04.04%
of	3	02.39%
and	4	02.03%
or	5	02.01%
for	6	01.81%
form	7	01.61%
from	8	01.58%
to	9	01.56%
enter	10	01.55%
if	11	01.43%
a	12	01.35%
on	13	01.28%
tax	14	01.09%
amount	15	01.06%
year	16	01.00%
you	17	01.00%
in	18	00.95%
income	19	00.83%
total	20	00.79%
your	21	00.74%

Table 5: Top 21 Most Frequent Words

segments. General details of the set are given in Tables 4 and 5 above.

The determiner '*the*', reputed to be the most frequent word in English (*OxfordDictionaries.com*), ranks only second in

---

[10] In this paper, we restrict ourselves to a general description of the methodology.

our form set. '*Line*' ranks first. Far from being a stopword, '*line*' is the basic structural and functional unit not only as a marker in the PDF layout of tax content, but as content-reference pointer and content holder.

The 21-top-ranked tokens offer a glimpse at tax-form activities. One can readily create a narrative—something along the lines wherein the text is about '*income*' and '*tax*' '*on/in*' '*forms*' and '*lines*' for some '*year*'. It concerns the reader '*you/your*' who is prompted to take action by '*enter*'ing '*amount*' and '*total*' ('*and, or*') when conditions are met ('*if, and, or*'). There is traffic of content '*from*' and '*to*'.

5.3 Terms as Text Instances of Tax Concepts and Entities

Multiword expressions (MWE) or terms are terminological units which denote concepts and entities in a domain. In the tax-and-regulations domain, terms can be compositional (Nunberg et al., 1994, Baldwin, 2006) in meaning and/or in form like '*timely estimated tax payment*'; others are not like '*married filing jointly*'; yet others are mixed instances of compositionality such as '*taxable sick leave pay*' or '*cannabis duty payable*'.

The domain-term lexicon is the result of the prior task of identifying, given the domain corpus, the domain-relevant concepts and entities by means of co-occurrence/collocation-based surface statistical measures. In addition, linguistic filters delete ill-formed term candidates from the final term list. We retain only nominal terms. Table 6 provides a breakdown for the number of MWE occurrences per segment.

Filing taxes requires understanding the concepts and entities being considered, i.e. what these MWE/terms denote in the tax-and-

Total No. of Segments		
41,660		
Total No. of Segments with		
0 MWE	23,496	57%
1 MWE	13,901	33%
2 MWE	2,901	7%
3 MWE	861	2%
4 MWE	287	.6%
> 4 MWE	194	.4%
Total No. of Segments that are MWE		
6,315		

Table 6: MWE Distribution

regulations domain. About 43.6% of all segments include at least one term. And about 35% of these

segments consist exactly of just terms. For instance, the segments '*net operating loss deduction*' or '*tentative income distribution deduction*' are the terms themselves.

The raw text in tax forms is fragmentary with a prevalence of nominal expressions; the fragmentation and its instantiation with nominal phrases mirror not only its function in the visual layout of the source documents but also the piecemeal cumulative reading and building of calculations.

5.4 Segment Type

Segment-type classification exploits the semantically-based features associated with the keys in the lexica. As the ultimate goal of our tax NLP system is to interpret and execute calculations expressed in the input as raw text, the preprocessor labels each segment according to the schema in Figure 2 below (each segment must be flagged with one of the bottom labels).

Segments that are labeled '*arithmetic operation*' have explicit verbs, nouns or adverbs that identify the operations; they also express complete operations like '*Subtract lines 13a plus 13b from line 12*'. '*Non-arithmetic operation*' segments either include quantity-oriented concepts like '*business expense*' as in '*Total unreimbursed employee business expenses*', or include references to quantities as in '*Total net gain from Schedule D (Form 1041), line 19, column (1)*'. We further divide '*amount*' segments into (i) term-based '*amount*' segments like '*Total unreimbursed employee business expenses*' and (ii) '*arithmetic operand*' segments that reference content in form-units to be used as input to a calculation as in '*Enter the amount from column (c) on line 1*'. Finally, '*non-arithmetic non-amount*' are classified as either '*particulars*', '*date*', '*description*', or '*declaration*' like for '*Social security number*' or '*I hereby...*'. Only segments labeled '*arithmetic operation*' and '*non-arithmetic operation amount*' are of interest in the context of the automatic extraction and execution of raw text calculations by an NLP system.

Details of the semantic-based segment-type breakdown are presented in Table 7. Over a fourth of all segments (28%), are clearly identifiable as '*arithmetic operations*' and '*arithmetic operand*'. In addition, more than half of the segments (57.5%) are about '*amount*' as concepts instantiated by tax terms. Currently, we do not discriminate among '*amount amount*' segments.

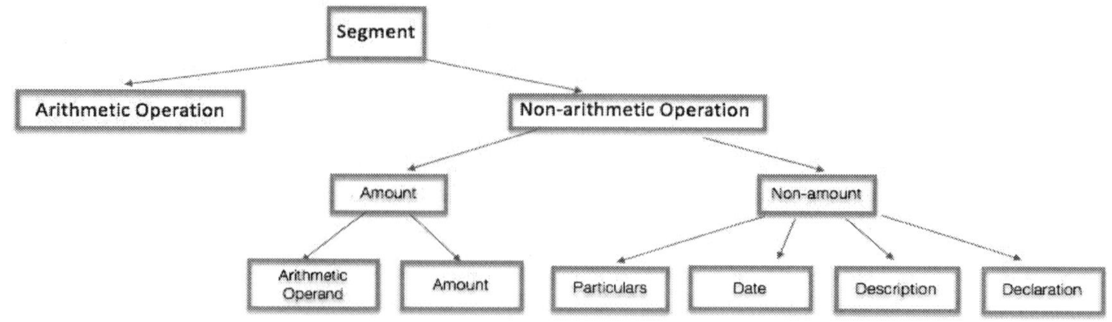

Figure 2: Semantic Segment-type Classification

Segment Total	Arithmetic Operations	Non-arithmetic Operations		Non-amount
		Amount		Non-amount
		Arithmetic Operand	Amount	
	3,970	7,687		
	11,657		23,940	6,063
41,660	28%		57.5%	14.5%

Table 7: Semantic Schema for Text Calculations

A subset of *'amount'* segments function as operands to in-progress calculations like *'enter total business expenses'*. Ideally, *'enter total business expenses'* should have a label indicative of its function—*amount operand*, to distinguish it from instances where the term *'total business expenses'* is, for example, part of an explanation.

5.5 Tense Marker

Due to the nature of the highly-formatted original PDF forms, many segments are verbless. The predominant table-like layout of tax forms encourages text fragments and isolated phrases. These segments identify, label, or prefix lines and line content. We use the absence/presence of a *'tense'* marker on the candidate head of a phrase to label segments.

Excluding non-amount segments (6,063) from the total number of segments (41,660), we have 35,597 segments relevant to calculations. Of these, 58% have a noun as the head of the topmost phrase and 42% have a verb as the root node. More than half of the tense-based segments are in the imperative mode as in *'Enter here and on Form 1041, line 25b'*, *'Itemize by charitable purpose'*, or *'If zero or less, enter 0 here, skip lines 13 through 21, and enter 0 on line 22'*. These commands are instructions that spell out the steps to take or not to build the calculations.

The breakdown for tensed versus non-tensed segments is in Table 8.

Non-tensed			Tensed		
Arithmetic Operation	Arithmetic Operand Amount	Amount	Arithmetic Operation	Arithmetic Operand Amount	Amount
470	5,042	15,228	3,510	3,017	8,330
20,740			14,857		

Table 8: Tense-Marker Frequency per Segment-Type

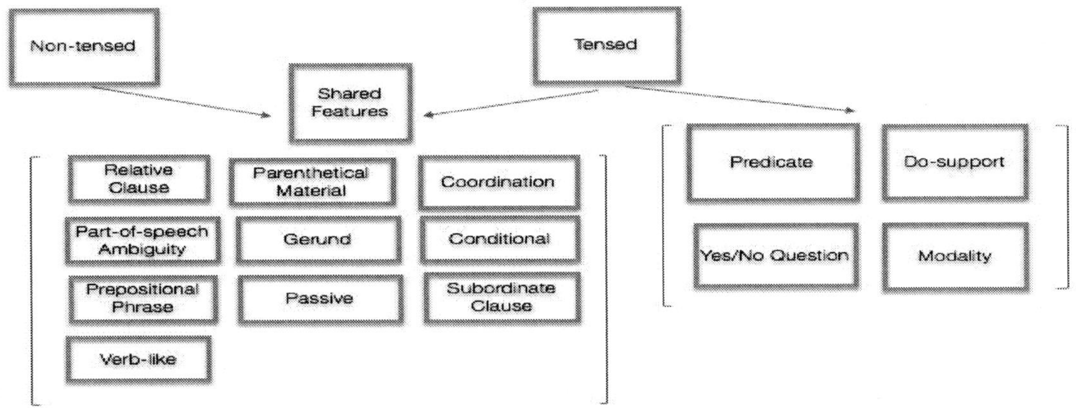

Figure 3: Linguistic Shared Features

5.6 The Structural Flavor of Segments

Automated phrase- and word-frequency lists based on the denotative classifications of parts of speech (POS) and lexical information in our lexica point to structural choices, which are used to label segments into smaller functional groups. The set of structural and functional labels that correspond to structural-syntactic instantiations in the collection of segments is shown in Figure 3. Before any deeper parsing, the labels serve as a precursor indication of the segment overall configuration.

For example, parenthetical material occurs in segments regardless of whether the segments are non-tensed as in *'ordinary income (loss) for schedule E'*, or tensed as in *'if you were a real estate professional, enter the net income or (loss) you reported.'* Arithmetic operations (in full or in part) can be contained inside parenthetical material like *'enter the result as a decimal (rounded to at least three places)'* or *'Add amounts in column (i), line 26'*. The intent of the parenthetical material needs to be weighed as it may or may not be relevant to calculations as in *'Other taxable disability income (see Help)'*. 16% of all segments have text in parentheses.

6 Can You Read Me Now?

A way of determining whether the language of income-tax forms is clear and simple is to measure the text set against readability indexes. Readability measures rely on various standardized writing components like sentence length (the shorter the better), word length (the shorter the better), concrete everyday language, active voice, no legalese or jargon, tabular presentation of complex information, etc.

Conveniently, Microsoft Word (version 16.27) comes with a readability tool. Running our text set as a collection of segments abstracted away from their position in the original highly-structured PDF yields a Flesch Reading Ease of 53.5 or a Flesch-Kincaid Grade Level of 8.8. With a grade of 8-9, the text set should be understood by 13- to 15-year-old individuals. In isolation, the language of tax-form segments appears on average clear and simple. Substantially, the language complies with *Plain Writing* principles.

However, readability measures and *Plain Writing* principles largely ignore the questions of how filers make sense of fragmented texts, of how each line relates to other lines in a cumulative reading process. More importantly, while they focus on lexes and the structures of phrases, these measures and *Plain Writing* principles disregard meaning and interpretation, i.e. to understand the text the filer must determine what the terms denote in the domain. Not a trivial reading task as 43% of all segments include at least one multiword term. For instance, the structure of and each of the words in the segment *'tax on lump-sum distributions'* are common, everyday language but what does *'lump-sum distributions'* denotes in the tax world?

One of the recommendations for writing clearly and simply is to use tabular presentation of complex information. Such display result in compressing content into fragments that can be displayed in table rows and headers. Such compression results in noun compounds and nominal phrases of varying complexity (58% in our set), which can make content less explicit. *Nominalizations* may be efficient for readers who are expert on or familiar with the tax-and-regulations domain, i.e. readers who can infer non-overt relations among concepts (and their token instantiations). These readers may be able to keep up (from line to line, from tax form to tax form) with the story on how to figure out their taxable income.

Finally, while the language of arithmetic operations expressed as text reads on average clearly and easily, understanding what the calculations consist in (operations and operands) can be challenging. Consider the following sequential segments; *'If line 27 is $186,300 or less ($93,150 or less if married filing separately for 2016), multiply line 27 by 26% (0.26). Otherwise, multiply line 27 by 28% (0.28) and subtract $3,726 ($1,863 if married filing separately for 2016) from the result.'* The Flesch-Kincaid Grade Level puts the above paragraph at 19.5, which is a level for skilled readers.

The complexity of some arithmetic operations along with concept and entity denotation in the tax domain may explain why only 10% of taxpayers file without any type of assistance.

7 Conclusion and Additional Questions

In this paper, we offer a first attempt at describing the language of income-tax forms. We viewed the task through a language analysis lens with no attempt at more logic-oriented semantic modeling. This approach also helps with the discovery of content and form that are idiosyncratic to the domain.

We discuss some basic syntactic and semantic patterns discovered through various statistical regularities across the segment set. The tabular presentation of content in the original PDF files has the effect of compressing the language resulting in a high number of noun compounds or multiword expressions wherein the relationships among concepts remain implicit as it is the case, for instance, with missing prepositions (*'living expenses'* with implicit preposition *'of'* versus *'distribution expenses'* with implicit preposition *'from'*.) Noun compounding can also introduce adjectival scope ambiguity. For example, is *'tentative'* a modifier of *'income'* or *'deduction'* in the expression *'tentative income distribution deduction'* as *'tentative income'* itself appears enough times across the tax-form set to be considered a MWE or tax concept?

Various labeling schemata, that incorporate our observations from descriptive statistics about income-tax forms, have been implemented to annotate raw segments automatically. This type of automatic annotation makes it easy to poke around segment sets (or any tax-form set, from tax year to tax year.)

A language-oriented description of how calculations or arithmetic word problems are displayed in the source PDF documents and expressed in raw text can help decide on the NLP approach and the level of analytic granularity best fitted to extract and to represent calculations so as to have these automatically interpreted and executed by downstream NLP components. For instance, is tense a linguistic feature necessary for the interpretation of calculations? What about modals? Should the structure of noun compounds and nominal phrases, a subset of which are instantiated by domain multiterm expressions, be made transparent? Is this level of granularity necessary for an automatic processing of calculations? While it may matter to human readers to have relations among members of complex nominal expressions explicitly stated to help understand tax-term-based calculations[11], it may be sufficient, i.e. *'clear and simple'*, for an NLP implementation to output accurate calculations by treating these expressions as opaque nominal singletons with no internal structure.

Acknowledgments

We thank Saikat Mukherjee and two anonymous reviewers for helpful comments.

References

Joo Jung An and Ned Wilson. 2016. *Tax Knowledge Adventure: Ontologies that Analyze Corporate Tax Transactions*, in *Proceedings of the 17th International Digital Government Research Conference on Digital Government Research*, Shanghai, China. June 08 2016. ACM, pages 303-311.

Timothy, Baldwin. 2006 . *Compositionality and multiword Expressions: Six of One, Half a Dozen of the Other?* In *Proceedings of the Workshop on Multiword Expressions: Identifying and Exploiting Underlying Properties*. Sydney, Australia. Association for Computational Linguistics, page 1. https://www.aclweb.org/anthology/W06-1201

---

[11] A topic worthy of some psycholinguistic experiments.

Joshua Blank and Leigh Osofsky. 2017. *Simplexity: Plain Language and the Tax Law*. In *66 Emory Law Journal 189*, pages 1-77. NYU Law and Economics Research Paper No. 16-17; University of Miami Legal Studies Research Paper No. 16-20

Stephen Cohen. 2005. *Words, Words, Words!!! Teaching the Language of Tax*. In *Georgetown Law Faculty Publications and Other Works*. 579. Pages 600-605.
https://scholarship.law.georgetown.edu/facpub/579

Michael Curlotti and Eric McCreath. 2011. *A Corpus of Australian Contract Language: Description, Profiling and Analysis*. In *Proceedings of the 13th International Conference on Artificial Intelligence and Law*. ACM, 2011.
http://dx.doi.org/10.2139/ssrn.2304652

Isabella Distinto, Nicola Guarina and Claudio Masolo. 2013. *A well-founded ontological framework for modeling personal income tax*. In *Proceedings of the Fourteenth International Conference on Artificial Intelligence and Law*. Rome, Italy. pages 33-42.

Ioannis Korkontzelos and Suresh Manandhar. 2010. Can recognising multiword expressions improve shallow parsing? In *Human Language Technologies: The 2010 Annual Conference of the North American Chapter of the Association for Computational Linguistics*, pages 636–644, Los Angeles, California, Association for Computational Linguistics

Geoffrey Nunberg, Ivan A. Sag, and Thomas Wasow. 1994. *Idioms*. In Stephen Everson, editor, *Language,* pages 491–538. Cambridge University Press.

Plain Writing Act Compliance Report, Internal Revenue Service. 2016.
https://www.irs.gov/pub/irs-pdf/p5206.pdf

Rachel Stabler. 2014. *What We've Got Here is Failure to Communicate: The Plain Writing Act of 2010*. In *Journal of Legislation*, Vol. 40, No. 2, pp. 280-323, 2014. https://ssrn.com/abstract=2574207

The Oxford English Corpus: Facts about the language. OxfordDictionaries.com. Oxford University Press. Archived from the original on December 26, 2011. Retrieved June 22, 2011.

Tone Analysis in Spanish Financial Reporting Narratives

Antonio Moreno-Sandoval[†,*], Ana Gisbert[‡], Pablo A. Haya[*], Marta Guerrero[*] and Helena Montoro[*,†]

[†]Laboratorio de Lingüística Informática, Autonomous University of Madrid
[‡]Accounting Department, Autonomous University of Madrid
[*]Instituto de Ingeniería del Conocimiento, Autonomous University of Madrid
{antonio.msandoval, ana.gisbert}@uam.es
{pablo.haya, marta.guerrero, helena.montoro}@iic.uam.es

This paper analyzes the tone (including polarity and semantic orientations) in a corpus of financial reports in Spanish. Specifically, we look at the Letter to Shareholders section of the Annual Reports, which focuses on an analysis of the financial performance, corporate strategies and other aspects relevant to investors. We use FinT-esp, a semantic analysis tool developed for Spanish narratives, based on lexicons and phrase-structure information. We divide the corpus in four subgroups based on the net earnings figure as a benchmark, to identify differences in tone between profit firms and loss firms. This paper confirms that Spanish financial narratives suffers a communicative bias towards positive terms (Pollyanna effect). Additionally, we provide a gold standard of financial narratives, based on a random selection of 1% of the sentences of the corpus of Letters. We run a first evaluation of three different sentiment analysis tools (Azure, Watson and FinT-esp) compared to the GS and observe that tone analysis in the financial narratives domain breaks with classical sentiment analysis (based on subjective feelings, value judgments, emotions). Financial narratives tone is linked to measurable facts and figures (financial results) and investors' expectations about the future performance of the firm.

1   Introduction

The last decade presents a unique scenario to extend new techniques in computational linguistics to understand financial narratives. The open access to a wide set of electronic resources of financial texts and the release of additional non-regulated disclosures (i.e. annual reports, earnings press-releases, conferences calls, earnings announcements) creates the perfect scenario to understand how managers make use of the language when communicating with stakeholders. Researchers in accounting and finance need to go beyond the use of manual textual analysis, traditional measures of readability and tone, or "bag-of-words". Computational linguistics and accounting academics must work aligned to advance in domain specific lists and new text mining techniques to understand the semantic orientation of sentences (Malo et al., 2014) and the use of the language to guide users' interpretations of financial texts (Malo et al., 2014; Loughran and McDonald, 2016).

Financial narratives are a central component of the companies' reporting package (Beattie, 2014). However, whereas quantitative disclosures (i.e. Financial Statements) are mostly regulated and subject to periodic controls by auditors and enforcement institutions, other financial and non-financial narratives (i.e. earnings press releases or environmental reports) are unregulated, unaudited and offer a wide degree of discretion to managers. The exponential increase of qualitative disclosures in the last decade has raised a wide debate on whether financial narratives really offer incremental information content on top of the traditionally regulated financial information (Boudt, Thewissen and Torsin, 2018; Plumlee et al., 2015). Managers choose between the use of narratives to increase transparency and reduce information asymmetry or intentionally bias investors' perceptions to obfuscate the reality about firm's performance (Merkl-Davis and Brennan, 2007; Arslan-Ayaydin et al., 2016).

Evidence shows that narratives are indeed value relevant, contribute to the company's reputation (Craig and Brennan, 2012) and investors and analysts decision making process (Boudt et al., 2018; Arslan-Ayayding et al., 2016; Yekini, et al., 2016). Therefore, computational linguistics can play a crucial role in supporting the accounting and finance field to discern about the use and orientation of financial narratives.

The first motivation for this study relies on the idea that company's earnings trend affects the tone of financial narratives. Particularly, for our research question, we investigate whether there are differences in the language orientation (opinion) of the letter to shareholders across benchmark vs. non-benchmark beating companies. We focus the empirical analysis on the letter to shareholders as a document with *"enormous rhetorical importance"* to build credibility and confidence about the company (Hyland, 1998) and influence investors' decisions (Baird and Zelin, 2000; Breton and Taffler, 2001).

Managers' choice to bias or enrich financial information depends on a set of incentives. Previous literature document significant capital market rewards (penalties) for benchmark (non-benchmark) beating companies (Graham et al. 2005). We consider these capital markets' rewards and potential penalties a clear incentive to manage upwards the tone of narrative disclosures, avoid negative messages and therefore, affect investors' perceptions about the performance of the firm. Previous literature in the US document that managers structure their narratives to manage investors' perceptions about the company performance (Alee and Deangelis, 2015). Li (2008) finds that firms with lower reported earnings have less readable annual reports (10-K) and more recently, Iatridis (2016), Davis and Tama-Sweet (2012) or Feldman et al. (2010), finds that benchmark beating, and high-growth firms tend to use less pessimistic language.

For a final sample of 76 companies listed in the Spanish Stock Exchange, we apply NLP techniques for tone analysis, and we measure the degree of accuracy of the use of these techniques in the domain of financial narratives.

The performance of current sentiment analysis (SA) systems seems less accurate when used in the financial domain compared to other narrative contexts as social media messages. We posit that the underperformance of the different tools is linked to the specific language complexity of financial narratives due to its impact on users' decisions that may affect the company's market value.

In spite of the caveats and limitations, this study is one of the first attempts to identify automatically the tone and semantic orientations of financial narratives in the Spanish language.

2   Characteristics of the corpus

The potential sample consists of 125 companies listed in the Madrid Stock Exchange. For each company, we accessed the corporate website in order to retrieve all the publicly available Annual Reports for the four-year period 2014-2017. However, the Spanish accounting regulation does not require the preparation of this document and therefore it is not available for all companies. We finally retrieved the Annual Reports dataset files in PDF format for a final sample of 76 reports.

Annual Reports have not a standardized format across companies, its content and structure vary significantly and therefore, they are rarely comparable documents. One of the few comparable sections across companies is the *Letter to shareholders*.

Due to the relevance of the "letter to shareholders", we focus the analysis on this specific and relevant section of the Annual Report. The letter to shareholders it is not subject to accounting regulation and it offers managers with a great opportunity to use their writing style to change investors' perceptions about the past, present and future performance of the company (Hooghiemstra, 2010). Previous literature documents that investors decisions are clearly influenced by the information presented in the letter to shareholders (Baird and Zelin, 2000; Breton and Taffler, 2001).

In order to identify differences in the language style across benchmark vs. non-benchmark beating companies, we group companies in groups based on the company's financial performance. For this purpose, we download financial data from ORBIS, a Bureau Van Dijk database with financial information for over 300 million companies across the Globe. ORBIS is key source of financial data for professional and academic use. More specifically, we download the net income figure (NI_{it}) for each sample company across the time-period 2013-2017 to classify firms in the following four groups as follows:

- **Group 1**: Companies reporting positive earnings (profits) ($NI_{it} > 0$) and improving past performance. That is, increasing earnings compared to the preceding year [$(NI_{it} - NI_{i,t-1})/ |NI_{it}| > 0$].

- **Group 2:** Companies reporting positive earnings (profits) ($NI_{it} > 0$) and declining past performance. That is, decreasing earnings compared to the preceding year $[(NI_{it} - NI_{i,t-1})/ |NI_{it}| < 0]$.
- **Group 3:** Companies reporting negative earnings (losses) ($NI_{it} < 0$) but improving past performance. That is, decreasing the amount of losses from the preceding year $[(NI_{it} - NI_{i,t-1})/ |NI_{it}|) > 0]$.
- **Group 4:** Companies reporting negative earnings (losses) ($NI_{it} < 0$) and declining past performance. That is, increasing losses compared to the preceding year $[(NI_{it} - NI_{i,t-1} / |NI_{it}|) < 0]$.

The initial corpus of the Letter to shareholders was composed of a total of 385 text, 462,189 words, 16,800 sentences, and 8,682 paragraphs (Moreno et al., 2019). However, we excluded from the final corpus those letters for companies with missing net income data in the ORBIS database (7 documents).

For the normalization of the corpus, each letter is in a separate file -encoded in UTF-8-, one sentence per line and double carriage return separating each paragraph.

The final 378 texts are distributed across the four groups as follows (Table 1):

	Num. of texts
Profits / Δ Earnings	258
Profits / ∇ Earnings	68
Losses / Δ Earnings	20
Losses / ∇ Earnings	32
Total	378

Table 1: Company classification and number of texts

3 Applying an opinion and semantic tool

Robo-readers (Malo et al., 2014) can extract opinion and semantic orientations from reports to identify how financial sentiments relate to future company performance. In this article, we apply a sentiment analysis engine to analyze the tone of a corpus of Spanish financial narratives. More specifically, instead of using informal texts in social media (see Section 4.2), we have focused the analysis on the sentiment and opinion in domain specific texts, Letter to shareholders.

We use a lexicon and rule-based sentiment engine instead of an ML classifier, with a general polarity lexicon and a phrased-structure grammar.

The domain-independent lexicon is made up of about 8,000 single word entries and more than 20,000 multiword expressions. The grammar is a modified version of the Spanish FreeLing (Padró and Stanilovsky, 2012). The grammar is used to identify semantic groupings at a phrase-structure level and to project polarity information up to the upper level. The label (Positive 100 to 1; Neutral 0; Negative -1 to -100) assigned to each sentence is the result of the projection of the different phrase units in the construction of the parsing tree (similar to the one described by Malo et al., 2014).

3.1 Preparing the corpus

The corpus consists of 16,800 sentences, but it includes lines for the names of Presidents/CEOs, their positions and section titles. To remove this irrelevant content for sentiment analysis, we delete all sentences with less than 4 words. The final corpus contains 14,812 sentences to run the opinion engine.

3.2 Output

We separate the final corpus into the four categories shown in Table 1. The opinion sentiment engine provides a numeric value for each sentence between -1 and 1, where 0 is the neutral value. Overall, the results clearly show that a positive opinion prevails in all categories (see Figure 1).

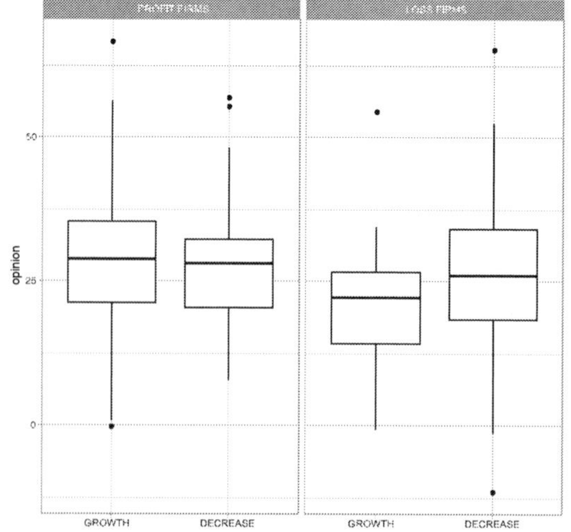

Figure 1: Opinion for the four categories

These results are consistent with expectations and previous literature that suggests the tendency of managers to present the analysis of the company's financial results from the best possible perspective. Figure 1 shows two remarkable results: (1) companies with losses and decreases in performance (group 4) have a higher positive tone compared to companies with losses but increases in performance (group 3); (2) Group 4 companies have a tone similar to group 1. That is, the worst performing companies maintain a positive tone similar to the best performing companies in the narratives of the letter to shareholders.

4   Results evaluation

In order to measure the performance of the opinion sentiment tool, we compiled a "Gold Standard" (FinT-esp GS) annotated by human experts.

4.1   Building an evaluation Gold Standard

The objective of the GS is to assess the accuracy of competing tools and observe the polarity distribution in the financial narratives domain.

Sample selection: We randomly selected 1% (148 sentences) of the sentences of the final corpus (14,812 sentences) as a significant representation of the complete dataset. Annotators tag a total of 130 sentences from profit companies and 18 sentences for companies with loss.

Annotation instructions: Annotators are informed about the requirement to assess the tone of the sentence from investor's perspective. This implies that the "referee" for disagreements between the two annotators must have financial knowledge:

- **Neutral**: statements without positive or negative judgements about the information (i.e. without adjectives and adverbs, such as "better", "increasingly", "significant", "unfortunately" etc.) Example: "*Nos dirigimos, un año más, a ustedes para informales sobre los resultados del ejercicio 2016 cuyas cuentas se someten a su aprobación*" (Trans. 'Once again, we are writing to inform you of the results for the fiscal year 2016, the annual accounts of which are submitted for your approval'). Additionally, sentences are considered neutral if includes the same amount of both positive and negative statements that compensate with each other and therefore, the tone of the message is neutralized. Conversely, if the number of positive statements predominates the sentence is considered as "positive", "negative"

otherwise. That is, when the number of negative statements predominates.

- **Positive**: "good news" messages based on real economic facts. Example: "*En Abril del 2017 tenía el placer de comunicarles un inicio de acuerdo con el fondo de pensiones APG para la creación de una Socimi especializada en activos residenciales.*" (Trans. 'In April 2017 I had the pleasure to inform you about the beginning of an agreement with the APG pension fund for the creation of a Real Estate Investment Trust specialized in residential assets').
- **Negative**: "bad news" messages or "positive" expressions that mask losses or decreases in earnings. Example: "*Esta presentación se produjo como consecuencia de la demora sufrida dentro del proceso negociador con el pool bancario en referencia a la reestructuración de la deuda.*" (Trans. 'This presentation occurred as a consequence of the delay in the negotiation process with the banking pool regarding debt restructuring')

Annotation guides have been created before the manual annotation from a sample of 1% of the dataset different from the one used in the GS.

Percent overall agreement = 80.41%
Free-marginal kappa = 0.71
Fixed-marginal kappa = 0.62

Table 2: Inter-annotators agreement

Annotators and "referee": Two expert linguists have tagged all 148 sentences independently. In addition, a financial expert has reviewed all the tone assessments and has decided the correct one in case of discrepancy between annotators. Only in few cases, based on her knowledge of the domain, the "referee" has corrected the annotations shared among linguists.

Table 2 shows the inter-annotator agreement for the 148 cases and 3 categories. Noteworthy is the fact that the annotators agreed more in the 130 sentences from the profit companies than in the 18 sentences from loss companies: 82.41% vs. 66.67%. The results are indicative of the difficulty of analyzing the tone of the narratives of companies with financial problems.

Following Fleiss's rule of thumb, kappa values from 0.40 to 0.75 are considered *"intermediate – good."* Therefore, the values obtained for the annotation procedure are quite satisfactory.

Finally, the financial expert's revision of the linguists' annotation makes the GS highly reliable for assessing the accuracy of the opinion analysis tools.

4.2 Semantic tone of the GS

Considering the GS a representative sample of the financial reporting domain, we focus on the distribution of polarity values. Results in Figure 2 show that the positive tone (70%) prevails over the others, with very few negative messages (8%).

These results contrast with the distribution of negative vs. positive tone in other highly studied domain: social media. Taking as a reference the TASS competition[1] developed between 2012 and 2017 for Sentiment Analysis in Spanish datasets, the InterTass2017 reports the following distribution for a Twitter GS with 1,625 tuits: 13% (neutral), 47% (+) and 40% (-) (see Figure 3). (Martínez-Cámara et al., 2017).

In Twitter, negative messages are close in number to positive messages. This great difference in polarity distribution forces sentiment systems to make a strong adaptation. The next section explains differences in performance across the three sentiment analysis tools: Watson, Azure, and our FinT-esp. Most tools are usually applied in sentiment analysis in social media (i.e. Twitter). Therefore, we could use to the values of the last competition InterTASS2017 as a reference for the state-of-the-art in Spanish (see Table 3)[2].

Best systems	M-F1	Acc.
ELiRF-UPV-run1	0.493	0.607
RETUYT-svm	0.471	0.596
ELiRF-UPV-run3	0.466	0.597

Table 3: Best systems in InterTASS 2017

5. Performance comparison of three sentiment tools

We have chosen two professional applications to evaluate their performance in an unusual domain.

Microsoft Azure Sentiment Analysis is included in the Text Analytics API service. It is based on machine learning algorithms and does not require training data. Azure uses neural network technology and word embeddings. The evaluation of each sentence has been done from the demo page[3] copying the results into a spreadsheet.

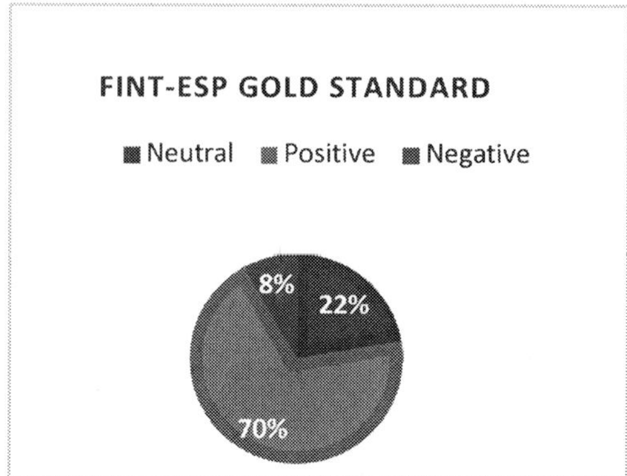

Figure 2: Polarity distribution in the Financial narratives

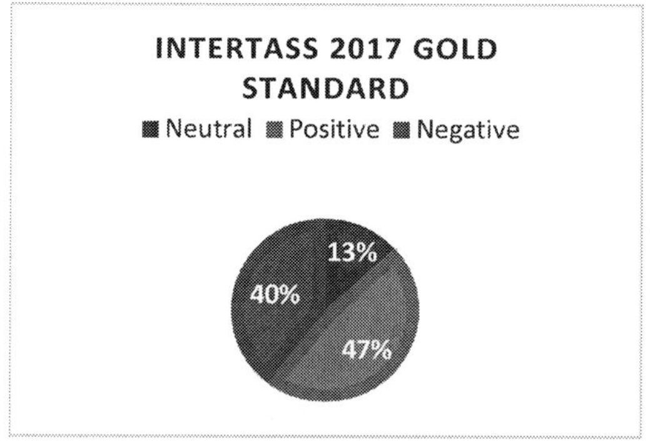

Figure 3: Polarity distribution in Twitter

IBM Watson NLU is a collection of APIs that offer text analysis through NLP[4]. We haven't created a custom model to get specific results that are tailored to the financial domain. In this way, we have maintained the same level of domain adaptation in all three systems. In the case of our lexicon-based system, we have not developed a specific one for financial terms.

---

[1] http://www.sepln.org/workshops/tass/
[2] All the systems participating in TASS 2017 "are based on the use of deep learning techniques as the state-of-the-art in SA in Twitter" (Martínez-Cámara et al. 2017).

[3] https://azure.microsoft.com/es-es/services/cognitive-services/text-analytics/
[4] https://natural-language-understanding-demo.ng.bluemix.net/

	Prec. N	Prec. +	Prec. -	Macro Prec.	Acc.	Recall N	Recall +	Recall -	Macro Recall	F1 N	F1 +	F1 -	M F1
Watson	0.26	**0.89**	**1.00**	**0.72**	0.43	**0.88**	0.32	0.08	0.43	0.41	0.47	0.15	**0.54**
Azure	**0.50**	0.73	0.33	0.52	**0.70**	0.06	**0.94**	**0.33**	0.45	0.11	**0.83**	**0.33**	0.48
FinT-esp	0.35	0.83	0.23	0.47	0.57	0.58	0.59	**0.33**	**0.50**	**0,44**	0,69	0,27	0.48

Table 4: Results against the FinT-esp Gold Standard

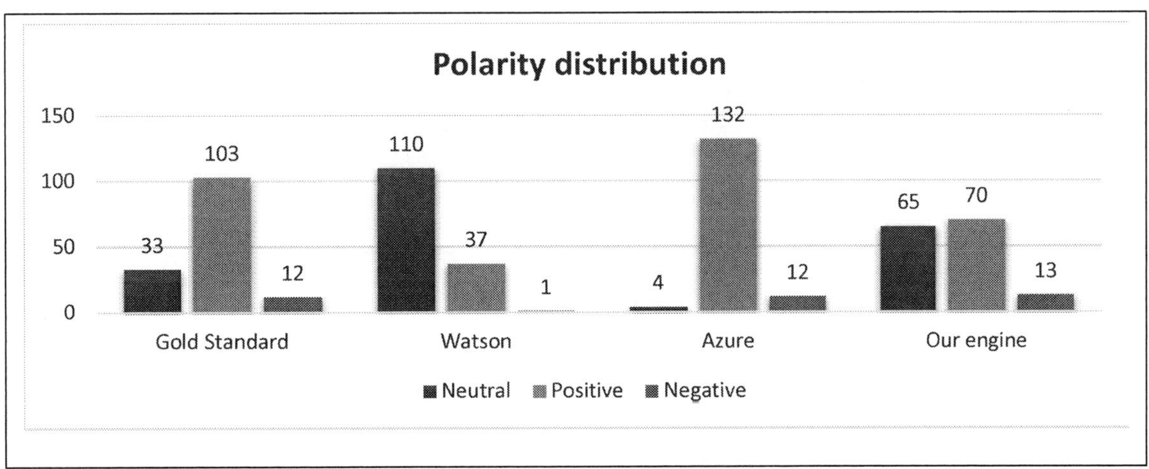

Figure 4: Polarity distribution in the FinT-esp GS and the three systems

Table 4 gives the detailed results of the evaluation, disaggregating the scores by polarity value. Figure 4 shows a wide variety in the performance of the systems, an indicator that each method uses very different technologies.

Azure approximates the distribution of the FinT-esp GS and obtains better results in Accuracy than the other systems (see Table 5). However, MacroF1 scores show that none of the 3 systems meets the objective of classifying the polarity of the sentences acceptably.

In the following section, we examine the peculiarities of the systems and the analyzed sentences.

5 Discussion

A general feature of the systems is that they provide very good precision results with positive sentences (from Azure 0.73 to Watson 0.89). However, in recall only Azure stands out (0.94). Bearing in mind that positive messages account for 70% of the GS, this largely explains why Azure wins in the benchmark (0.83 F1 score for +).

Conversely, Azure is the worst at detecting neutrals (F1 score of 0.11). None of the three systems works acceptably with negative messages either (F1 between 0.15 and 0.33).

Systems	M-F1	Acc.
ELiRF-UPV-run1	0.49	0.61
Watson	**0.54**	0.43
Azure	0.48	**0.70**
FinT-esp	0.48	0.57

Table 5: Macro F1 and Accuracy

None of the three systems has been specifically trained for the financial reporting domain. Therefore, it is striking, that each has a very different analysis strategy. Watson is decidedly inclined towards neutral messages, while Azure bets almost exclusively on interpreting sentences as positive. The contingency table displays the distribution of the variables (Table 6).

Watson and Azure are based on ML technology, whereas FinT-esp is based on a general polarity lexicon and phrase rules. In the test results, the distribution of positives and neutrals is similar. In all three systems, the focus is on the subjective part of the texts and not on the description of the facts. Something that escapes all the tools evaluated here.

FinT-esp			
GS	negative	neutral	positive
negative	3	4	5
neutral	3	23	7
positive	7	38	58

Azure			
GS	negative	neutral	positive
negative	4	0	8
neutral	4	2	27
positive	4	2	97

Watson			
GS	negative	neutral	positive
negative	1	11	0
neutral	0	29	4
positive	0	70	33

Table 6: Contingency tables

Next, we will show an example of each polarity, where none of the three systems has been able to analyze correctly.

- **Negative**: "*Seguimos siendo líderes, pero nuestro mercado ha quedado reducido al 20% del total.*" (trans. 'We are still leaders, but our market has been reduced to 20% of the total'). From the investor's point of view, the strong reduction in the market share is considered as bad news. Azure and the Fin-tesp system classified the sentence as positive, probably because of the presence of "leaders."

- **Positive**: "*La deuda a diciembre de 2016 se redujo en los últimos doce meses de 305 millones a 188 millones de euros, es decir, hemos bajado 117 millones de euros en un año.*" (Trans. 'Debt at December 2016 was reduced in the last twelve months from 305 million euros to 188 million euros, in other words, we have reduced 117 million euros in one year'). Although "debt" is an inherently negative word, the message is positive for investors, as the debt has been drastically reduced. Watson and the FinT-esp tool classified the sentence as neutral; Azure as negative.

- **Neutral**: "*A pesar de todo ello, la eficiencia de la actividad en una sola planta se fue poniendo de manifiesto a lo largo del año.*" (Trans. 'In spite of all this, the efficiency of the activity in a single plant became evident throughout the year'). In this sentence two opposite movements are neutralized, expressed by "in spite of" and by "efficiency". Azure and the FinT-esp tool classified the sentence as positive. Watson as neutral.

These examples reflect the argumentative complexity of financial narratives. It is common for two opposing ideas to appear in the same sentence. In some cases, they are neutralized but in others one is stronger than the other.

6 Conclusions and future work

Financial narratives have boosted across the last decade, offering a unique setting to test different computational linguistics methodologies for sentiment analysis across a specific language domain: financial reporting texts. Additionally, whereas most of the current studies have been centered in English financial narratives, the access to non-English financial and non-financial qualitative disclosures offers a great opportunity for sentiment analysis in other languages.

This paper confirms that the Spanish financial narrative suffers the Pollyanna effect (Rutherford 2005). That is, a communicative bias towards positive terms. This bias is consistent with the managers' aversion to communicate bad news that may affect the company's capital market value or the company's reputation. The positive bias in the narratives affects the accuracy of the different semantic analysis tools. Compared to the use of SA techniques in other narrative contexts as the social media, differences in the performance of the three tested systems suggests that the specific language complexity of these texts requires more domain-specific methods for tone analysis. Particularly, across bad-performing companies where sentences including words such as "debt" or "restructuring" can be misclassified as "negative" whereas the overall context of the message is positive. Or bad news related to decreases in performance can be masked with the use of positive expressions (i.e. *we are still leaders, although our market has been reduced to 20% of the total*).

Additionally, the different distribution of polarity in two gold standards is consistent with

Chen, Huang and Chen (2018) who showed that there is a clear difference in the language of "market sentiment of social media data" compared to other "formal reports". In the financial reporting domain, the tone is directly linked to measurable facts (financial performance, sales and gross margin increases, debt reductions, EBITDA), past performance and investors' future expectations about the company. Therefore, while expectations can be measured with classic sentiment analysis, measuring financial facts needs the participation of financial experts to create specialized lexicons, train models and offer a neat assessment of those sentences that present discrepancies. This explains why the three tools evaluated had poor results.

Žnidaršič et al. (2018) have studied the importance of the expressions of "trust" and "doubt" in financial communications, and the correlations with the financial activity of companies. An extension of this article will address lexical and terminological issues based on the FinT-esp corpus.

We contribute to language resources with the compilation of the first corpus of "letters to shareholders" in Spanish. Additionally, we create a gold standard (and the corresponding annotation guidelines) to evaluate opinion systems and we have carried out a first sentiment analysis comparison. Both the corpus and the GS will be freely available to researchers on the project site.

Future work aims to develop a financial polarity lexicon, including verbs and adverbs expressing epistemic modality (probability and certainty) as suggested in Malo et al. (2014). We will also explore Machine Learning methods trained on dataset to classify the tone of financial narratives.

Acknowledgments

This research is supported by Spanish Ministry of Economy and Industry, via the FinT-esp project (TIN2017-89351-R).

References

Kristian D. Allee and Matthew D. Deangelis. 2015. The structure of voluntary disclosure narratives: evidence from tone dispersion. *Journal of Accounting Research*. 53 (2): 241-274. https://doi.org/10.1111/1475-679X.12072

Özgür Arslan-Ayaydin, Kris Boudt and James Thewissen. 2016. Managers set the tone: Equity incentives and the tone of earnings press releases. *Journal of Banking and Finance*, 72 (Supplement): S132-S147. https://doi.org/10.1016/j.jbankfin.2015.10.007

Jane E. Baird and Robert C. Zelin II. 2000. The effects of information ordering on investor perceptions: An experiment utilizing presidents' letters. *Journal of Financial and Strategic Decisions*, 13(3): 71-81.

Gaétan Breton and Richard J. Taffler 2001. Accounting information and analyst stock recommendation decisions: a content analysis approach. *Accounting and Business Research*, 31 (2): 91-101. https://doi.org/10.1080/00014788.2001.9729604

Vivien Beattie, 2014. Accounting narratives and the narrative turn in accounting research. *The British Accounting Review*, 46(2): 111-134. https://dx.doi.org/10.1016/j.bar.2014.05.001

Kris Boudt, James Thewissen and Wouter Torsin. 2018. When does the tone of earnings press releases matter? *International Review of Financial Analysis*, 57: 231-245. https://doi.org/10.1016/j.irfa.2018.02.002.

Chung-Chi Chen, Hen-Hsen Huang and Hsin-Hsi Chen. 2018. NTUSD-Fin: A Market Sentiment Dictionary for Financial Social Media Data Applications. In *Proceedings of the LREC 2018 Workshop "The First Financial Narrative Processing Workshop (FNP 2018)"*. Miyazaki, Japan, pages 59–65

Russell J. Craig and Niamh M. Brennan. 2012. An exploration of the relationship between language choice in CEO letters to shareholders and corporate reputation. *Accounting Forum*. 36 (3): 166-177. https://doi.org/10.1016/j.accfor.2012.02.004.

Angela K. Davis and Isho Tama-Sweet. 2012. Managers' use of language across alternative disclosure outlets: earnings press releases versus MD&A. *Contemporary Accounting Research*, 29 (3): 804-837. https://doi.org/10.1111/j.1911-3846.2011.01125.x

Ronen Feldman, Suresh Govindaraj, Joshua Livnat and Benjamin Segal. 2010. Management's tone change, post earnings announcement drift and accruals. *Review of Accounting Studies* 15(4):915-953. https://doi.org/10.1007/s11142-009-9111-x

John R. Graham, Campbell R. Harvey and Shiva Rajgopal. 2005. "The economic implications of corporate financial reporting", *Journal of Accounting and Economics*, 40(1-3): 3-73. https://doi.org/10.1016/jacceco.2005.01.002

Reggy Hooghiemstra, 2010. Letter to the shareholders: A content analysis comparison of letters written by

CEOs in the United States and Japan, *The International Journal of Accounting*, 45(3): 275-300. https://doi.org/10.1013/j.intacc.2010.06.006

Ken Hylan. 1998. Exploring corporate rhetoric: Metadiscourse in the CEO's letter. *Journal of Business Communication*, 35(2): 224-245. https://doi.org/10.1177/002194369803500203

George E. Iatridis. 2016. Financial reporting language in financial statements: Does pessimism restrict the potential for managerial opportunism? *International Review of Financial Analysis*, 45(1): 1-17. https://doi.org/10.1016/j.irfa.2016.02.004.

Feng Li. 2008. Annual Report Readability, Current Earnings, and Earnings Persistence. *Journal of Accounting and Economics*, 45(2-3): 221-247. https://doi.org/10.1016/j.acceco.2008.02.003.

Tim Loughran and Bill McDonald. 2016. Textual Analysis in Accounting and Finance: A survey. *Journal of Accounting Research*, 54 (4): 1187-1230. https://doi.org/10.1111/1475-679X.12123.

Pekka Malo, Ankur Sinha, Pekka Korhonen, Jyrki Wallenius and Pyry Takala. 2014. Good Debt or Bad Debt: Detecting Semantic Orientation in Economic Texts. *Journal of the Association For Information Science And Technology*, 65(4): 782-796. https://doi.org/10.1002/asi.23062

Eugenio Martínez-Cámara, Manuel C. Díaz-Galiano, M. Ángel García-Lumbreras, Manuel García-Vega and Julio Villena-Román. 2017. Overview of TASS 2017. In *Proceedings of TASS 2017: Workshop on Semantic Analysis at SEPLN*, September 2017, pages 13-21. https://www.researchgate.net/publication/3204102 70

Doris M. Merkl-Davis and Niamh M. Brennan. 2007. Discretionary disclosure strategies in corporate narratives: incremental information or impression management? *Journal of Accounting Literature*, 27: 116-196.

Antonio Moreno-Sandoval, Ana Gisbert and Helena Montoro. 2019. FinT-esp: a corpus of financial reports in Spanish. Presented at the *XI International Conference on Corpus Linguistics*, Valencia, Spain, 15-17 May 2019 (to be published as a chapter).

Lluis Padró and Evgeny Stanilovsky. 2012. FreeLing 3.0: Towards Wider Multilinguality. In Proceedings of LREC 2012 2473-2479. http://hdl.handle.net/2117/15986

Marlene Plumlee, Darrell Brown, Rachel M. Hayes and R. Scott Marshall. 2015. Voluntary environmental disclosure quality and firm value: Further evidence. *Journal of Accounting and Public Policy.* 34(4): 336-361. https://doi.org/10.1016/j.accpubpol.2015.04.0004

Brian A. Rutherford. 2005. Genre Analysis of Corporate Annual Report Narratives: A Corpus Linguistics-Based Approach. *Journal of Business and Communication,* 42(4): 349-378. https://doi.org/10.1177/0021943605279244

Liafisu S. Yekini, Tomasz P. Wisniewski, Yuval Millo. 2016. Market reaction to the positiveness of annual report narratives. *The British Accounting Review.* 48 (4): 415-430. https://doi.org/10.1016/j.bar.2015.12.001

Martin Žnidaršič, Jasmina Smailović, Jan Gorše, Miha Grčar, Igor Mozetič and Senja Pollak. 2018. Trust and Doubt Terms in Financial Tweets and Periodic Reports. In *Proceedings of the LREC 2018 Workshop "The First Financial Narrative Processing Workshop (FNP 2018)"*. Miyazaki, Japan, pages 59–65.

The FinTOC-2019 Shared Task:
Financial Document Structure Extraction

Rémi Juge[*]
Fortia Financial Solutions
Paris, France

Najah-Imane Bentabet[*]
Fortia Financial Solutions
Paris, France

Sira Ferradans
Fortia Financial Solutions
Paris, France

`name.surname@fortia.fr`

Abstract

In this paper, we present the results and findings of The FinTOC-2019 Shared Task on structure extraction from financial documents. This shared task was organized as part of Second Financial Narrative Processing Workshop, collocated with the 22nd Nordic Conference on Computational Linguistics (NoDaLiDa'19) Conference. The shared task aimed at collecting systems for extracting table of contents from Financial prospectuses by detecting the document titles and reorganizing them in a hierarchical way. The FinTOC shared task is the first to target the task of Table of content extraction in the domain of Finance.

1 Introduction

Long document comprehension is still an open problem in Natural Language Processing (NLP). Most of the corporate information or academic knowledge is locked in long documents (> 10 pages) with complex semantic and layout structure. Documents are generally converted into plain text and processed sentence by sentence, where the only structure that is easily identified are the paragraphs, thus loosing the internal organization of the document. Despite the importance long document analysis, there are few available resources and none in a low resource domain such as the finance.

In this shared task, we focus on extracting the table-of-contents (TOC) of financial prospectuses that are official pdf documents in which investment funds precisely describe their characteristics and investment modalities. The majority of prospectuses are published without a TOC which is of fundamental importance for sophisticated NLP tasks such as information extraction or question answering on long documents. Although the content they must include is often regulated, their format is not standardized and displays a great deal of variability ranging from plain text format, towards more graphical and tabular presentation of data and information, making the analysis of the discourse structure even more complicated.

In this paper, we report the results and findings of the FinTOC-2019 shared task.[1] The Shared Task was organized as part of Second Financial Narrative Processing Workshop, co-located with the 22nd Nordic Conference on Computational Linguistics (NoDaLiDa'19) Conference.[2]

A total of 6 teams submitted runs and contributed 4 system description papers. All system description papers are included in the FNP 2019 workshop proceedings and cited in this report.

2 Previous Work on TOC extraction

We find mostly two approaches. The goal of the first approach is to parse the hierarchical structure of sections and subsections from the TOC pages embedded in the document. Most of the research developed in this area has been linked to the INEX [1] and ICDAR competitions [2, 3, 4] which target old and long OCR-ised books instead of small papers. These documents are very different from the documents that we target in this shared task, charaterized by having complex layout structure (see Fig. 1 for some examples). Outside these competitions, we find the methods proposed by El-Haj et al [5, 6, 7], based also in TOC page parsing.

In the second approach, we find methods that detect headings using learning methods based on layout and text features. The set of titles are hierarchically ordered according to a predefined rule-based function [2, 8, 9]. Recently, we find methods

---

[*]Both authors contributed equally to this work

[1]`http://wp.lancs.ac.uk/cfie/fnp2019/`
[2]`http://wp.lancs.ac.uk/cfie/`

Figure 1: Random pages from the investment document data set. We observe that the title organization and, in general, the layout is complex.

that address TOC extraction as a sequence labelling task to which deep learning methods can be applied [10].

3 Task Description

As part of the Financial Narrative Processing Workshop, we present a shared task on Financial Document Structure Extraction.

Systems participating in this shared task were given a sample collection of financial prospectuses with a wide variety of document structures and sizes. The goal was to automatically process them to extract their document structure. In fact the task was decomposed into two subtasks:

- **Title detection**: The document is splitted into text blocks (a text block regroup lines that have the same layout and that are spatially close to each others) extracted from financial prospectuses by our in-house parser. Each text block needs to be classified as a 'title' or 'non-title'. As shown in Fig. 2 the titles can have different layouts (marked with red and green boxes) and they have to be distinguished from the regular text ('non-title' with grey boxes).

- **TOC extraction**: In this subtask, the goal is to (i) identify the hierarchical level of the titles, for instance, in Fig. 2, the text in green bounding boxes are hierarchically at the same level and at a different level than the title in red, (ii) organize the titles of the document according to the hierarchical structure to produce the final TOC. Again in Fig. 2, the system needs to identify that the red tagged heading is hierarchically above than the green ones.

It is important to note that two titles, with the same layout and the same text can have different hierarchical levels depending on their location in the document.

All participating teams were provided a common training data set for subtask 1 which included the original pdfs, the xml versions of the pdfs obtained using the Poppler[3] library, and a csv file containing, for each text block, a set of layout features and binary labels indicating if the text block is a title or not. For the second subtask, the training data set also included a TOC of the documents in the xml format proposed by ICDAR competitions[2]. A blind test set was used to evaluate the output of the participating teams.

As stated in Section 2, most of the previous research on TOC generation has been confined to short papers such as research publications (*Arxiv* database), or standard documents such as digitalized books. However, the task of extracting the TOC of commercial documents with a complex layout structure in the domain of finance is not much explored in the literature.

4 Shared Task Data

Next, we discuss the corpora used for the title detection and TOC extraction subtasks.

4.1 Corpus annotation

Financial prospectuses are available online in a pdf format and are also made available from asset managers. We compiled a list of 58 prospectuses from Luxembourg written in English to create the

---

[3] poppler.freedesktop.org

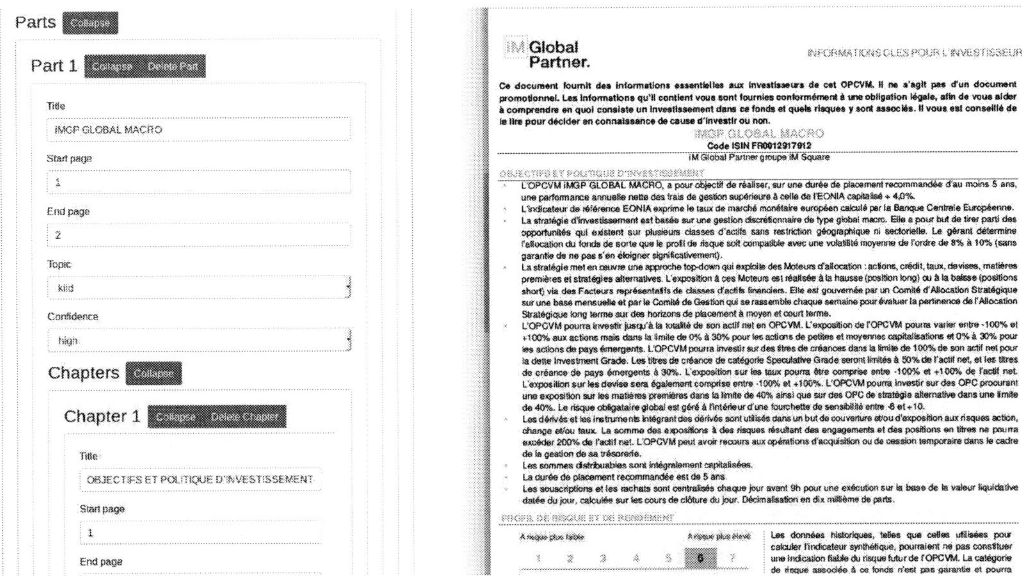

Figure 2: Screenshot of the annotation tool developed internally.

data sets of the subtasks. We chose prospectuses with a wide variety of layouts and styles.

	Xerox F1	Inex08 F1
tagger 1 & tagger 2	93.8%	87.5%
tagger 1 & reviewer	96.7%	92%
tagger 2 & reviewer	96.8%	93.5%

Table 1: Agreement scores between different annotators of the investment document data set.

We provided three annotators with the original pdfs and an internally developed web tool that produces a hierarchical *json* file containing each TOC-entry together with some features (title, starting-page, ending-page and children). Each annotator was ask to:

1. Identify the title: Locate a title inside the pdf document.

2. Associate the entry level in the TOC: Every title must have an entry level in the TOC of the document with the following constraints 1) high level entries cannot be inside lower level entries (i.e. a *Part* cannot be inside a *Chapter*), 2) the entries levels must be successive (i.e. after a *chapter* we have a *section* not a *subsection*).

3. Add title: Copy-paste the title text directly into a web form, see Fig. 2 label *Title*

The predefined type of entry levels for the TOC were *Part*, *Chapter*, *section*, *subsection* or *para-graph*, that could be inside the *Front matter*, *Body matter* or *Back matter*. Therefore, the maximum TOC level was 5.

Each document was annotated independently by two people and a third person would review the annotations to resolve the possible conflicts. The agreement scores between annotators are depicted in Table 1. We can observe high agreement scores, allowing us to be confident enough about the quality of our data set.

Annotation Challenge: Headings identification Investment prospectuses are commercial documents whose complex layout aims at highlighting specific information such that a potential investor can identify it quickly. Hence, annotating a title and its level in the TOC hierarchy is a difficult task as one cannot rely on the visual appearance of the title to do so. Some examples can be observed in Fig. 3 and Fig. 4.

Annotation Challenge: Tagging pdf documents. The annotation of pdf documents is not evident since they are meant to be used for display. The tool we developed for the annotations does not allow annotators to directly annotate on the pdf and thus they had to manage two different platforms at the same time. Working this way is prone to mistakes.

Annotation Challenge: Matching annotations and text blocks. Our internal tool uses a copy-paste mechanism to create the TOC entries, intro-

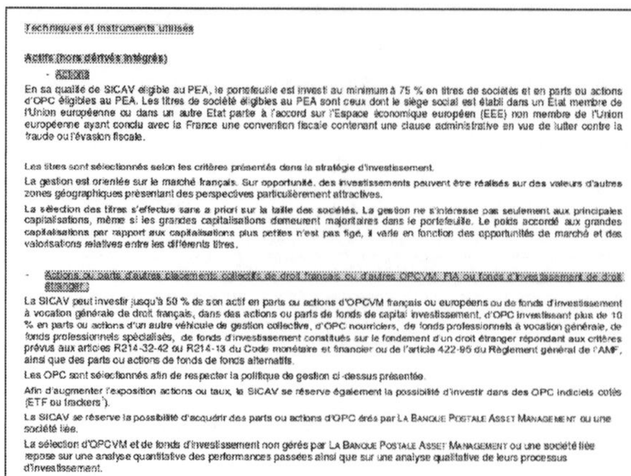

Figure 3: Page from a prospectus with the titles selected coloured boxes. An example where title identification is not evident because titles can have the same style as regular text.

Figure 4: Page from a prospectus with the titles selected coloured boxes. An example where title identification is not evident because titles may expand a part of a line.

ducing some noise at the string level. On the other hand, we extract text from the pdf using an automatic pdf to xml process. For the data set creation, each title annotation had to be matched to a text block. This pipeline introduces noise in the final csv.

4.2 Corpus Description

In the following, we provide an analysis of the data used for the shared task. For both subtasks, the released training sets were the same excepted that for subtask 2, an additional xml file (*groundtruth[...]max_depth=5.icdar2013.xml*) at the ICDAR format was given. The reason for it is twofold: it gave to the participants the output format that they had to respect for the submissions and allowed them to participate in subtask 2 without having a title extraction system from subtask 1.

In the csv files available to the participants, each text block came with a set of layout features: *is_bold, is_italic, is_all_caps, begins_with_cap, be-*

gins_with_numbering and page_number and its source xml file. Some statistics on this data set are presented in Table 2.

number of documents	58
average number of pages	90
number of text blocks	90441
number of titles (% of text blocks)	14%
begin_with_numbering (% of text blocks)	20%
is_bold (% of text blocks)	18%
is_italic (% of text blocks)	1.3%
is_all_caps (% of text blocks)	20%
begins_with_cap (% of text blocks)	68%
level 1 (% of titles)	7%
level 2 (% of titles)	26%
level 3 (% of titles)	33%
level 4 (% of titles)	30%
level 5 (% of titles)	4%

Table 2: Statistics on the investment document data set.

5 Participants and Systems

	# teams	# std runs
subtask 1	5	10
subtask 2	2	3
papers	5	-

Table 3: Statistics on the participation in the two subatsks.

A total of 24 teams registered in the shared task from 18 different institutions, and 6 teams participated with standard runs and 5 submitted a paper with the description of their method, see Table 4 for more information about their affiliation. In Table 3, we show the details on the submissions per task. It is important to note that not all the participants that submitted a standard run, sent a paper describing

Team	Affiliation	Tasks
Daniel [11]	STIH, Sorbonne Université	1 and 2
FinDSE [12]	Faculdade de Engenharia da Universidade do Porto	1
UWB [13]	University of West Bohemia	1
YseopLab [14]	Yseop	1
IHSMarkit	IHS Markit	2
Aiai	OPT, Inc	1

Table 4: List of the 6 teams that participated in Subtasks of the FinTOC Shared Task.

their approach.

Participating teams explored and implemented a wide variety of techniques and features. In this section, we give a brief description of each system, more details could be found in the description papers appearing in the proceedings of the FNP 2019 Workshop.

Daniel [11]: The only team to submit to both subtasks and a paper. Their approach for the Fin-TOC title detection task assumed the presence of a TOC page which they detect by identifying the page numbers that are aligned at the right of the page. Then, they extract each TOC entry using regular expressions and construct the hierarchical structure of the TOC with a rule-based method based on indentation and multi-level numbering.

FinDSE [12]: They addressed the FinTOC Title detection as a sentence classification task. They added to the provided features (see Section 4.2 for more details) some others such as morphological (number of characters distributed into categories), semantic (contains date) and linguistic features (predetermined tokens such as 'appendix', 'annex', etc, part-of-speech of the first word, ...). Their best performing model used an extra-tree classifier. It is interesting to note that, according to their experiments, adding predetermined tokens actually reduced the performance of the final method.

UWB [13]: Only the FinTOC Title detection was addressed in this paper. As for the other methods, they state the problem as a binary classification of text sentences, for which they use a Maximum entropy classifier, on top of a diverse set of features. In addition to the provided characteristics, they add others related to style (font size, font type size), orthographic descriptors, and char n-grams.

YseopLab [14]: The authors tackle only the Fin-TOC Title detection task. Similarly to other participants, they first try to design an additional set of features to feed an SVM classifier. Then, unlike previous methods, they run two separated experiments where they use a character-level CNN and a word-level BiLSTM with attention to extract semantic features from text blocks and classify them.

Aiai [15]: This team proposes the use of word2vec word-embeddings followed by a LSTM and BiLSTM, respectively for run 1 and 2, see Table 5. Then, they add an attention layer. Finally,

they train several times the same model and do ensembling as a last step.

6   Results and Discussion

Evaluation Metric   For the first subtask, the participating systems are ranked based on the weighted F1 score obtained on a blind test set (official metric). Table 5 reports the results obtained on Fin-TOC title detection task by the teams detailed in the previous section.

Team	F1 score
Aiai_2	**0.982**
Aiai_1	0.98
UWB_2	0.972
YseopLab_2	0.9716
FinDSE_1	0.970
FinDSE_2	0.968
UWB_1	0.965
Daniel_1	0.949
Daniel_2	0.942
YseopLab_1	0.932

Table 5: Results obtained by the participants for the first FinTOC task. The teams are ordered by the weighted F1 score.

Regarding the FinTOC TOC extraction subtask, the metric is based on the official title-based measure of the ICDAR 2013 competition on book structure extraction [2] (ICDAR'13 measure from now on). More specifically, the final F1 score is the mean of the InexF1 score and the Inex level accuracy. For the results on this task, please check Table 6.

Team	ICDAR'13 measure
Daniel_1	**0.427**
IHSMarkit_1	0.39
IHSMarkit_2	0.388

Table 6: Results obtained by the participants for the FinTOC TOC extraction task. The teams are ordered by the ICDAR'13 measure (see the text for more details).

Discussion.   A surprising fact of the reported methods is that the best performing methods (Aiai_1 and Aiai_2 with 0.98, UWB-2 with 0.972 and YseopLab_2 with 0.9716 F1 score) have radically different approaches. Team UWB-2 does not use deep learning methods. Instead, they add meaningful features to a maximum entropy classifier and they show through ablation tests that all features are important to attain their result. On the other hand, the best performing system of YseopLab_2 implements character-level CNN with no hand-engineered features. Finally, both methods of Aiai use (Bi-)LSTMs with attention mechanisms on top of word embeddings. For the second task, only one paper was submitted describing Daniel_1 team's method, which proposed a rule-based approach to title hierarchization.

In their paper [12], the team FinDSE performs a set of experiments with a wide variety of features. An interesting conclusion is that the usage of common first words from titles such as *Annex* or *Appendix* can be counter productive. This contradicts the methods commonly used in the literature [16, 17, 18, 19]. Moreover, it shows the difficulty of transferring state-of-the-art methods trained on public datasets to commercial documents such as financial prospectuses.

7 Conclusions

In this paper we presented the setup and results for the FinTOC-2019 Shared Task:Financial Document Structure Extraction, organized as part of the Second Financial Narrative Processing Workshop, collocated with the 22nd Nordic Conference on Computational Linguistics (NoDaLiDa'19) Conference. A total of 24 people registered from 18 different institutions. 6 teams participated in the shared task with a wide variety of techniques.

We introduced a new data set on the TOC extraction problem in text automatically extracted from pdf files in English. This scenario is very realistic in everyday applications which may explain the participation of public universities and profit organizations from the financial domain.

Acknowledgments

We would like to thank our dedicated annotators who contributed to the building of the corpora used in this Shared Task: Anais Koptient, Aouataf Djillani, and Lidia Duarte.

References

[1] Bodin Dresevic, Aleksandar Uzelac, Bogdan Radakovic, and Nikola Todic. Book layout analysis: Toc structure extraction engine. In Shlomo Geva, Jaap Kamps, and Andrew Trotman, editors, *Advances in Focused Retrieval*, pages 164–171, Berlin, Heidelberg, 2009. Springer Berlin Heidelberg.

[2] Antoine Doucet, Gabriella Kazai, Sebastian Colutto, and Günter Mühlberger. Icdar 2013 competition on book structure extraction. In *Document Analysis and Recognition (ICDAR), 2013 12th International Conference on*, pages 1438–1443. IEEE, 2013.

[3] Thomas Beckers, Patrice Bellot, Gianluca Demartini, Ludovic Denoyer, Christopher M. De Vries, Antoine Doucet, Khairun Nisa Fachry, Norbert Fuhr, Patrick Gallinari, Shlomo Geva, Wei-Che Huang, Tereza Iofciu, Jaap Kamps, Gabriella Kazai, Marijn Koolen, Sangeetha Kutty, Monica Landoni, Miro Lehtonen, Véronique Moriceau, Richi Nayak, Ragnar Nordlie, Nils Pharo, Eric Sanjuan, Ralf Schenkel, Xavier Tannier, Martin Theobald, James A. Thom, Andrew Trotman, and Arjen P. De Vries. Report on INEX 2009. *Sigir Forum*, 44(1):38–57, June 2010. Article disponible en ligne : http://www.cs.otago.ac.nz/homepages/andrew/papers/2010-4.pdf.

[4] Thi Tuyet Hai Nguyen, Antoine Doucet, and Mickael Coustaty. Enhancing table of contents extraction by system aggregation. In *Proceedings of the International Conference on Document Analysis and Recognition, ICDAR*, 2018.

[5] Mahmoud El Haj, Paul Rayson, Steven Young, and Martin Walker. *Detecting document structure in a very large corpus of UK financial reports*. LREC'14 Ninth International Conference on Language Resources and Evaluation. Proceedings of the Ninth International Conference on Language Resources and Evaluation (LREC-2014) . European Language Resources Association (ELRA), Reykjavik, Iceland, pp. 1335-1338, 2014.

[6] Mahmoud El Haj, Paul Edward Rayson, Steven Eric Young, Paulo Alves, and Carlos Herrero Zorita. *Multilingual Financial Narrative Processing: Analysing Annual Reports in English, Spanish and Portuguese*. World Scientific Publishing, 2 2019.

[7] Mahmoud El-Haj, Paulo Alves, Paul Rayson, Martin Walker, and Steven Young. Retrieving, classifying and analysing narrative commentary in unstructured (glossy) annual reports published as pdf files. *Accounting and Business Research*, pages 1–29, 2019.

[8] Caihua Liu, Jiajun Chen, Xiaofeng Zhang, Jie Liu, and Yalou Huang. Toc structure extraction from ocred books. In *International Workshop of the Initiative for the Evaluation of XML Retrieval*, pages 98–108. Springer, 2011.

[9] Abhijith Athreya Mysore Gopinath, Shomir Wilson, and Norman Sadeh. Supervised and unsupervised methods for robust separation of section titles and prose text in web documents. In *Proceedings of the 2018 Conference on Empirical Methods in Natural Language Processing*, pages 850–855, 2018.

[10] Najah-Imane Bentabet, Rémi Juge, and Sira Ferradans. Table-of-contents generation on contemporary documents. In *Proceedings of ICDAR 2019*.

[11] Gael Lejeune Emmanuel Giguet. Daniel fintoc-2019 shared task: Toc extraction and title detection. In *The Second Workshop on Financial Narrative Processing of NoDalida 2019*, 2019.

[12] Henrique Cardoso Carla Abreu and Eugénio Oliveira. Findsefintoc-2019 shared task. In *The Second Workshop on Financial Narrative Processing of NoDalida 2019*, 2019.

[13] Tomas Hercig and Pavel Král. Uwbfintoc-2019 shared task: Financial document title detection. In *The Second Workshop on Financial Narrative Processing of NoDalida 2019*, 2019.

[14] Anubhav Gupta Hannah Abi-Akl and Dominique Mariko. Fintoc-2019 shared task: Finding title in text blocks. In *The Second Workshop on Financial Narrative Processing of NoDalida 2019*, 2019.

[15] Ke Tian and Zi Jun Peng. Finance document extraction using data augmented and attention. In *The Second Workshop on Financial Narrative Processing of NoDalida 2019*, 2019.

[16] Anoop M Namboodiri and Anil K Jain. Document structure and layout analysis. In *Digital Document Processing*, pages 29–48. Springer, 2007.

[17] Alan Conway. Page grammars and page parsing. a syntactic approach to document layout recognition. In *Document Analysis and Recognition, 1993., Proceedings of the Second International Conference on*, pages 761–764. IEEE, 1993.

[18] Florendia Fourli-Kartsouni, Kostas Slavakis, Georgios Kouroupetroglou, and Sergios Theodoridis. A bayesian network approach to semantic labelling of text formatting in xml corpora of documents. In *International Conference on Universal Access in Human-Computer Interaction*, pages 299–308. Springer, 2007.

[19] Koji Nakagawa, Akihiro Nomura, and Masakazu Suzuki. Extraction of logical structure from articles in mathematics. In *International Conference on Mathematical Knowledge Management*, pages 276–289. Springer, 2004.

FinTOC-2019 Shared Task: Finding Title in Text Blocks

Hanna Abi Akl
Yseop
`habi-akl@yseop.com`

Anubhav Gupta
Yseop
`agupta@yseop.com`

Dominique Mariko
Yseop
`dmariko@yseop.com`

Abstract

As part of FNP Workshop Series, "Title Detection" is one of the two shared tasks proposed on Financial Document Structure Extraction. The objective of the task was to classify a given text block, that had been extracted from financial prospectuses in pdf format, as a title. Our DNN-based approach scored a weighted F1 of 97.16% on the test data.

1 Introduction

The Portable Document Format, also known as pdf, is an electronic document format from Adobe Inc. Launched in early 1990s, this format has now become the de-facto means of sharing information across the Internet. However, given the lack of "basic high level logical structure information" (Chao and Fan, 2004), the process of layout and content extraction from a pdf is difficult. The obstacles in extracting information from a pdf, as enumerated by Hu and Liu (2014), are:

- absence of information regarding structure

- disagreement of the render order with the "reading order"

- overlap of object blocks

- myriad layouts and fonts

Consider the process of automating the information extraction from financial documents. Not being able to recognize where a paragraph begins or ends in a financial report can be a strain on many levels: a) it not only blurs important information, but b) can also be misleading in decisions taken based on said report. Though a number of open-source and commercial tools are available, the goal of establishing correctly a semantic unit (paragraphs, tables) and ascertaining its role (title,

header) is far from being complete (Bast and Korzen, 2017).

The **FinTOC-2019 Shared Task: "Financial Document Structure Extraction"** (Juge et al., 2019) of **Financial Narrative Processing Workshop** comprises two shared-tasks:

- Title detection

- TOC structure extraction

In this paper, we propose and evaluate three methods to detect titles (Shared Task 1). Since text comes in many different formats, this problem can become exponentially heavy to treat. For that purpose, our experiment is concerned with identifying only titles in pdf reports.

2 Experiments

Our first approach was to use a standard SVM classifier (Cortes and Vapnik, 1995) to understand the data and evaluate their non-linearity. The second and third approaches are based on deep learning classifiers. The second design is inspired by a BiLSTM recurrent neural network (RNN) model with attention (Zhou et al., 2016). The third model is a convolutional neural network (CNN) with character embedding (Zhang et al., 2015).

2.1 Data

The training data was extracted from 44 documents using the Poppler utility libraries (popplerutils) and converted into xml files. The contents of the xml were transformed into a csv file with the help of various heuristics by the organisers. The resulting file had 75 625 text blocks and 7 features describing each of them. Since these features were automatically generated they were noisy. For example, some of the text blocks that begin with determiner such as 'a', dates and addresses were erroneously marked as *begins_with_numbering*. Even though the original pdf files were provided we decided to work only with the provided xml and csv files because a) the result needed to be submitted in the provided csv format and b) the heuristic to transform xml into text blocks (as presented in csv) was unknown.

2.2 Approach

The first model we evaluated was a SVM classifier. It was trained on a combination of features, compiled from the existing features presented within the original csv file as well as additional features extracted from pre-processing work on the xml files (similar to format and linguistic features of Hu et al. (2006)). These features capture layout and form of the text, which can play a deciding part in the classification. In addition to the provided features, we computed:

1. **top:** integer indicating the placement of the text with respect to the top of the document page

2. **left:** integer indicating the placement of the text with respect to the left of the document page

3. **width:** integer indicating the horizontal space occupied by the text

4. **height:** integer indicating the vertical space occupied by the text

5. **font:** integer indicating the size of the text

6. **number of dots:** integer indicating the total number of dots in the text

7. **is last character dot:** binary indicating if the text ends with a dot (1) or not (0)

8. **count of capital letters:** integer indicating the total number of capital characters in the text

9. **character count:** integer indicating the total number of characters in the text

10. **word count:** integer indicating the total number of words in the text

11. **average word length:** float indicating the average number of characters per word in the text

12. **number count:** integer indicating the total number of digits in the text

13. **count of words in capital:** integer indicating the total number of capitalized words in the text

14. **similarly avg word length:** integer indicating average token length

15. **cnn output** binary prediction provided by the CNN model (described later).

The observed variance and results were very close with and without the CNN outputs added as input features, so after evaluation of the noise in the features (as predictors), we decided to foster two deep learning approaches based on raw text entries and to focus on regularisation methods to prevent high variance observed in the SVM results.

The second model is a BiLSTM–Attention model relying on word embedding. It has 2 dense layers, each composed of 64 neurons and is deployed with a batch size of 256 and 100 epochs. The purpose of this method is to evaluate the possible semantic composition of sentences (as predictors) and how relevant they are for the task. It contains five components:

1. **Input layer:** inputs text to the model

2. **Embedding layer:** parses text into words and maps each word into a low dimension vector

3. **LSTM layer:** makes use of BiLSTM to get high-level features from the previous step

4. **Attention layer:** produces a weight vector, and merges word-level features from each time step into a sentence-level feature vector, by multiplying the weight vector

5. **Output layer:** uses the sentence-level feature vector for classification

The aim of this architecture is to make use of the attention mechanism, which can automatically focus on the words that have a decisive effect on classification (in this case, the heavy constituents of a title), to capture the most important semantic information in a text block, circumventing the question of noise in the feature set. The

Experiment	Model								
	BiLSTM-ATTENTION			CNN			SVM		
Hardware	Intel Core i7 2.20GHz 16GB RAM NVIDIA GeForce GTX 1050 Ti 4Go			Intel Core i7 2.20GHz 16GB RAM NVIDIA GeForce GTX 1070 8Go			Intel Xeon 3.70GHz 64GB RAM 8 CPU cores		
	F1 (home) (%)	F1 (lboard) (%)	RunTime (hrs)	F1 (home) (%)	F1 (lboard) (%)	RunTime (hrs)	F1 (home) (%)	F1 (lboard) (%)	RunTime (hrs)
Experiment 1	96.02	91.24	7-9	-	-	-	95.96	91.13	2-4
Experiment 2	94.04	93.18	7-9	95.03	97.16	1-2	-	-	-

Table 1: Comparative table of results provided for leaderboard

hyper-parameter selection follows the findings of (Zhou et al., 2016) for the neural network. The number of layers, batch size, number of epochs, and learning rate have all been picked from a referenced model which achieved competitive results against state-of-the-art networks. The sequence length has been chosen to match the number of characters in the longest sentence. We also used dropout to regularize the network and alleviate over-fitting. Between experiments 1 and 2, we increased the number of hidden units from 32 to 64 to improve the accuracy of the model.

The third model is a CNN classifier. The purpose of this method is to evaluate the combinatorics of characters at word level (as predictors) and how relevant they are for the task. A state-of-the-art competitive word-level character embedded convolution network is used. The model follows the conclusion of Zhang et al. (2015) for tackling small dimensional problems: integrating both upper-case and lower-case letters in set of predictors might improve the results in case the data set is small (AG news case). This consideration was reinforced by the intuition that identifying both small and capital characters was relevant for the Title detection task, which was confirmed by comparing between the results driven from differentiating between upper and lower cases and the those driven by lower-case only. From a dictionary of all characters included in the training set, a character embedding operation is performed on all sentences. Word-level character embedding size of 175 is chosen for this transformation and sentences are turned into a matrix of embedded characters. This matrix is then fed to the CNN, which has the following characteristics:

1. **Convolution layers**: 2D convolution (4 convolution layers)

2. **Pooling layers**: 1D convolution reducing dimensions

3. **Fully connected layers**: transformation providing the prediction from softmax probabilities.

4. **Parameters selection**: In order to reduce the variance while training, we used a standard dropout of 0.5 at each epoch. Augmenting or reducing the dropout has showed worse results. We also added a cross validation step from a set of 1500 individuals, evaluated every ten epoch, the best epoch in this evaluation range was then chosen to become the warm start for the next 10 epochs. The number of layers chosen is the best trade off we found between a deeper network, our GPU computational capacity and runtime. The model was trained on 100 epochs, but converges quickly towards epoch 40, which eventually provided the best results.

2.3 Evaluation

For the given training data set, approximately 1 in 6 text blocks was a title. Thus, it was a case of class imbalance. A classifier which labels every text block as 'non-title' scored a weighted F1 of **80.12 %**. Our objective was to improve this score.

The performance of the three models on train and leaderboard sets are listed in Table 1. In this Table, the scores we obtained locally (F1 (home)) are compared with the final score on competition test set (F1 (lboard)). The experiment 1 corresponds to the results sent by the first deadline and the second one refers to the extended deadline submission. As the Deep Learning models originally had been trained on different GPU, we also added a comparative table on the model with best performances (CNN) with same architecture and parameters as the one provided for leaderboard results, so the influence of the architecture is clarified (Table 2).

	CNN Model		
	AUC (train) (%)	F1 (home) (%)	RunTime (hrs)
Intel Core i7 2.20GHz 16GB RAM NVIDIA GeForce GTX 1070 8Go	91.41	95.03	1-2
Intel Core i7 2.20GHz 16GB RAM NVIDIA GeForce GTX 1050 Ti 4Go	90.99	95.01	5

Table 2: Compared results for CNN, GPU dependent

3 Related Works

Most of the literature deals with extraction of information from scientific documents since they are publicly available and in large quantity. Gao et al. (2011) exploited common typesetting practice (Style Consistency of page Components) in books to extract structural information from pdf documents. Their solution was based on weighted bipartite graphs and optimal matching based on Kuhn-Munkres algorithm. A similar approach was used by Klampfl et al. (2014) to analyse the structure of scientific articles. They defined a heading as a text block that appears, in reading order, before a **main** text block. Other defining features of a heading, according to them, are:

- starts with a number or a capital letter

- consists of at least one non-whitespace letter

- has at most 3 lines

- font size is not less that of surrounding text blocks

- distance to the text block is not more than a given level

According to Constantin et al. (2013), the differentiating feature of a title is font frequency. In other words, since titles occur less frequently in a document their font will also be rare with respect to other fonts present in the document.

Most of the works that process financial documents focus on obtaining tabular data from the files. Potvin et al. (2016) employs rectilinear search algorithm and Chen et al. (2017) makes use of rectangle mining (REMINE).

In summary, almost every approach utilizes the geometric data available in pdf files to analyse and extract their content.

4 Conclusions

We proposed three different approaches to tackle the problem of title identification. Designing and working with different architectures allows room for improvement. For the BiLSTM-Attention model, depth can be experimented with by adding more layers and invigorating existing layers with more neurons. Of course, a subliminal challenge here would be accommodating the necessary hardware and supplying enough computational power to run such model in a reasonable time. For the CNN model, there are many possibilities in experimenting by acting on each component separately and fine-tuning its hyper-parameters, trying to optimize the network for small dimensional sets. We have not tried initializing the weights with a specific distribution yet and though the number of possible convolutions is limited by our GPU capacity, we believe there is room for performance improvement optimising the convolution graphs to precisely fit the memory capacities on larger GPU. Another path would be to consider this task as a computer vision one and try the CNN to detect graphical areas related to titles from PDF images.

Finally, it would also be interesting to build on our efforts to examine and rank features by importance and study the most influential features on the title classification exclusively. That trail might bring up interesting patterns worth exploring and possibly even replicating over other NLP tasks.

References

Hannah Bast and Claudius Korzen. 2017. A benchmark and evaluation for text extraction from pdf. In *Proceedings of the 17th ACM/IEEE Joint Conference on Digital Libraries*, JCDL '17, pages 99–108, Piscataway, NJ, USA. IEEE Press.

Hui Chao and Jian Fan. 2004. Layout and content extraction for pdf documents. In *Document Analysis Systems VI*, pages 213–224, Berlin, Heidelberg. Springer Berlin Heidelberg.

Xilun Chen, Laura Chiticariu, Marina Danilevsky, Alexandre V. Evfimievski, and Prithviraj Sen. 2017. A rectangle mining method for understanding the semantics of financial tables. In *14th IAPR International Conference on Document Analysis and*

Recognition, ICDAR 2017, Kyoto, Japan, November 9-15, 2017, pages 268–273.

Alexandru Constantin, Steve Pettifer, and Andrei Voronkov. 2013. Pdfx: Fully-automated pdf-to-xml conversion of scientific literature. In *Proceedings of the 2013 ACM Symposium on Document Engineering*, DocEng '13, pages 177–180, New York, NY, USA. ACM.

Corinna Cortes and Vladimir Vapnik. 1995. Support-vector networks. *Machine Learning*, 20(3):273–297.

Liangcai Gao, Zhi Tang, Xiaofan Lin, Ying Liu, Ruiheng Qiu, and Yongtao Wang. 2011. Structure extraction from pdf-based book documents. In *Proceedings of the 11th Annual International ACM/IEEE Joint Conference on Digital Libraries*, JCDL '11, pages 11–20, New York, NY, USA. ACM.

Jianying Hu and Ying Liu. 2014. *Analysis of Documents Born Digital*, pages 775–804. Springer London, London.

Yunhua Hu, Hang Li, Yunbo Cao, Li Teng, Dmitriy Meyerzon, and Qinghua Zheng. 2006. Automatic extraction of titles from general documents using machine learning. *Information Processing Management*, 42(5):1276 – 1293.

Rémi Juge, Najah-Imane Bentabet, and Sira Ferradans. 2019. The fintoc-2019 shared task: Financial document structure extraction. In *The Second Workshop on Financial Narrative Processing of NoDalida 2019*.

Stefan Klampfl, Michael Granitzer, Kris Jack, and Roman Kern. 2014. Unsupervised document structure analysis of digital scientific articles. *International Journal on Digital Libraries*, 14(3):83–99.

Benoit Potvin, Roger Villemaire, and Ngoc-Tan Le. 2016. A position-based method for the extraction of financial information in PDF documents. In *Proceedings of the 21st Australasian Document Computing Symposium, ADCS 2016, Caulfield, VIC, Australia, December 5-7, 2016*, pages 9–16.

Xiang Zhang, Junbo Zhao, and Yann LeCun. 2015. Character-level convolutional networks for text classification. In *Advances in neural information processing systems*, pages 649–657.

Peng Zhou, Wei Shi, Jun Tian, Zhenyu Qi, Bingchen Li, Hongwei Hao, and Bo Xu. 2016. Attention-based bidirectional long short-term memory networks for relation classification. In *Proceedings of the 54th Annual Meeting of the Association for Computational Linguistics (Volume 2: Short Papers)*, pages 207–212, Berlin, Germany. Association for Computational Linguistics.

Daniel@FinTOC-2019 Shared Task : TOC Extraction and Title Detection

Emmanuel Giguet
Normandie Univ, UNICAEN,
ENSICAEN, CNRS, GREYC
14000 Caen, France
emmanuel.giguet@unicaen.fr

Gaël Lejeune
STIH, EA 4509
Sorbonne University
75006 Paris, France
gael.lejeune@sorbonne-universite.fr

Abstract

We present different methods for the two tasks of the 2019 FinTOC challenge: Title Detection and Table of Contents Extraction. For the Title Detection task we present different approaches using various features : visual characteristics, punctuation density and character n-grams. Our best approach achieved an official F-measure score of 94.88%, ranking 6 on this task. For the TOC extraction task, we presented a method combining visual characteristics of the document layout. With this method we ranked first on this task with 42.72%.

1 Introduction

This paper describe our participation to the FinTOC-2019 Shared Task dedicated to Financial Document Structure Extraction (Rémi Juge, 2019). We submitted results for the two sub tasks: *Title detection*, a binary classification task focusing on detecting titles in financial prospectuses, and *TOC structure extraction* aiming at identifying and organizing the headers of the document according to its hierarchical structure.

Title detection and Table of Content (ToC) extraction are two important tasks for Natural Language Processing and Document Analysis, in particular in the context of digital libraries and scanned books. ToC extraction aims to retrieve or create a ToC in documents where the logical structure is not explicitly marked, difficult to detect or "computationnaly opaque" (de Busser and Moens, 2006). ToC extraction enriches the access to searchable text, in particular in the domain of digital humanities in which the texts are usually longer than in other domains involving Information retrieval (IR) and Natural language Processing (NLP). Rich logical structures is exploited for instance for document classification and clustering (Doucet and Lehtonen, 2007; Ait Elhadj et al., 2012).

Title detection can be a preliminary task for ToC extraction since it will help to detect a page with an existing ToC or it can help to find the bricks to reconstruct the ToC. It can also help classification systems which rely on titles and text structure to detect salient information in textual data(Lejeune et al., 2015). Salient sentences detection can as well be improved via text structure information (Denil et al., 2014).

In section 2 we will give a brief presentation of existing techniques for ToC extraction and title detection tasks. We will present our systems[1] in section 3 and Section 4 will be dedicated to conclusion and perspectives.

2 State of the Art

Textual data is often described as "unstructured data" as opposed to structured data like databases or XML data for instance. However, it is probably more accurate to describe textual data as "computationnaly opaque" so that only the file format can be qualified structured, unstructured or semi-structured. The logical structure of natural language data is probably more important for human understanding than the syntactic structure. For instance, in press articles important information is found in the titles and subtitles, making the detection of titles important for improving web indexation (Changuel et al., 2009) or downstream NLP tasks (Huttunen et al., 2011; Daille et al., 2016; Tkaczyk et al., 2018). Regarding title detection task itself, (Xue et al., 2007) showed that for web pages, the size of the characters is not enough to detect titles but (Beel et al., 2013) showed to the contrary that for PDF document it is the best heuristic (70% accuracy).

Visual and textual information can be combined

---

[1]Code source available online : https://github.com/rundimeco/daniel_fintoc2019

to make a difference between title and non titles, as in boilerplate removal (Lejeune and Zhu, 2018; Alarte et al., 2019).

There are two main types of ToC extraction techniques: those relying on the detection of ToC pages and those relying on the book content. The ICDAR Book Structure Extraction competitions results (Doucet et al., 2013) showed that the most promising systems are hybrid ones, (Nguyen et al., 2017) showed how combining multiple systems can lead to significant improvements in the results. As in boilerplate detection and removal, geometric relations and font information form the main feature types for ToC extraction (Klampfl et al., 2014).

3 Methods and Results

3.1 TOC Extraction

In order to participate to this first edition and to deliver results in a very short time, we made quite strong assumptions and some shortcomings. Our strategy relies on the detection of the Table of Content (ToC). A simple fallback strategy based on the whole content analysis is used when no ToC pages are detected.

In previous INEX Book Structure Extraction Competitions, we used to consider only the whole document to extract the structure (Giguet and Lucas, 2010a,b; Giguet et al., 2009). Taking into account the whole content of the document has many advantages. First, it allows to handle documents without ToC. Second, it permits to extract titles that are not included in the ToC, such as lower-level titles or preliminary titles. Thus, it reflects the real structure of the document. Third, and not the least, it avoids having to manage or to process erroneous ToCs. Indeed, the ToC of a document may not be synchronized with the actual version of the document when the author forget to update it. It may also contain entries that are not titles, for instance a paragraph incorrectly labelled as a title, or wrong page numbers. Those cases are not rare.

Although these issues are well known and plead in favor of an extraction from the whole content, it is interesting to work with a different approach. Thus we choose to locate ToC pages, to extract their content, and to submit the result as the document structure. Our expectations is to have a good precision but a low recall due to missing or incomplete ToCs.

3.1.1 Technical assumptions

The experiment is conducted from PDF documents to ensure the control of the entire process. The document content is extracted using the `pdf2xml` command (Déjean, 2007).

We assume that the PDF reports are automatically generated by the PDF driver of a word processor. Thus, we do not check if the document is a scanned document or if it is the output of an OCR application. Consequently, we do not consider possible trapezoid or parallelogram distortion, page rotation or curved lines. This assumption simplifies the initial stages: baselines are inferred from the coordinates on the x-axis; left, right and centered alignments are inferred from the coordinates on the y-axis.

We also assume that PDF drivers serialize the content of a page area by area, depending on the page layout. A content area corresponds to a page subdivision such as a column, a header, a footer, or a floating table or figure. When a content area is processed, we assume that characters and lines are serialized in reading order, so that there is no ordering problem to consider. Thus, when parsing a page, we expect to find the ToC entries serialized in reading order, and we expect to find the different parts of each ToC entry serialized in reading order.

However, content areas are represented neither in the PDF structure nor in the `pdf2xml` output. Content area are implicitly inferred by the cognitive skills of the reader. Moreover content areas can be serialized in many ways in the PDF. For instance, header and footer areas can be serialized before the document body area. The boundary delimitation of content areas inside a page is one of the main challenges.

Bounding the ToC areas over pages is not straight due to the absence of marks that separate them from other adjacent areas. In our process, positional information of headers and footers are inferred from the document structure in order to help the boundary delimitation of ToC areas. Taking into account the consistency of the styles within the ToC, and the style contrast with other parts should also help the delimitation.

We point out that there is no concept of "word" or "number" or "token" in PDF. In order to ease the processing, `pdf2xml` introduces the concept of "token", a computational unit based on character spacing. In practice, output tokens correspond to words or numbers, what we can expect, but they can also correspond to a composition of several interpretable unit (e.g., "Introduction....5" or a breakdown of an interpretable unit (e.g., "C" "O" "N" "T" "E" "N" "T").

3.1.2 Locating the ToC pages

The ToC is located in the first pages of the document. It can spread over a limited number of contiguous pages. In the training set, we observed in practice up to three contiguous pages.

While observing various ToCs, it appears that few properties are common to all ToCs over the collection. Some ToCs have a title, others don't have it. Some ToCs have section numbering, others don't have it. One formal property is common to all ToCs we observed in the corpus: the page numbers of a ToC are *right-aligned* and form an increasing sequence of integers.

These characteristics are fully exploited in the core of our ToC identification process: we consider the pages of the first third of the document as a search space. Then we select the first right-aligned sequence of lines ending by an integer and that may spread over contiguous pages. We do not have to bound the expected number of ToC pages.

3.1.3 Building ToC entries

A ToC Entry is made of several parts, namely an optional level number, the title, an optional leader line (i.e., dotted line), and the page number. A regular expression is enough to capture the different part of the expected ToC entry. This process must be applied with care since there is a significant risk of confusion between two cases:

- long titles may spread over multiple lines, up to two lines in the corpus,

- major headings may not be associated to page numbers. Their page number is implicit and usually corresponds to the page number of the following subheading. For instance, when the title of a chapter is not specified in a ToC, its page number is the same as the page number of its first section.

Styling and span information helps managing these cases. Leader lines are optional and may not be present on all ToC entries, in particular on major headings. While leader lines ease the association between titles and page number when title is short or line spacing is thin, larger line spacing, eventually combined to larger font-sizes, can be enough to ease the association for the reader.

3.1.4 Inferring the Hierarchy

A ToC is a hierarchical structure. From a computational point of view, it can be seen as the result of a preorder depth-first tree traversal. In practice, it is not the case since we deal with natural language, not computational structure: all the titles do not have to be mentioned. It is the case for lower-level subheadings which could significantly burden the synthetic overview. It is also the case for the main title, or for unnamed parts, such as preliminaries, which are defined by their position and may be considered as minor parts.

A combination of contrastive effects usually reflects the hierarchy:

- larger *line-spacing* can be used to highlight major headings ;

- positive *indentation* can be used to indicate lower-level subheadings;

- *formatting character effects* such as bold, italic, character case and font-size can be used: smaller font-sizes or lower case for lower-level subheadings; bold or uppercase for higher-level headings;

- *numbering character sets*: uppercase letters (e.g., A, B, C, I, II) are more often used for numbering higher-level headings while lowercase letters (e.g., a, b, c, i, ii, iii, α, β, γ) are used for lower-level subheading;

- *multi-level numbering structure*: subheading numbering (e.g., a, b, c) can be prefixed by parent numbering (e.g., A.2.a, A.2.b, A.2.c). The numbering of major parts, such as chapter (e.g., A), may not be prefixed in subheading multi-level number (e.g., 2.a, 2.b, 2.c) and may remain implicit.

Heading numbering may be prefixed by a functional term, such as Appendix, Chapter, Article, etc. It has to be handled. No specific list of terms has to be build. The term is repeated at the beginning of several ToC entries, before the heading number: it is enough to handle it.

In our process, the computation of the hierarchical structure is based on the combination of subheading indentation and multi-level numbering structure of ToC entries.

	Run	F-measure
Daniel	1	42.72
IHSMarkit	1	39.41

Table 1: Results for the ToC Generation Task (test set)

| Xrx-measure Links | | | | Title | |
Doc	Prec	Rec	F1	Acc	book id
0	97.7	48.6	64.9	84.5	1252823262
1	87.2	51.9	65.1	96.5	1139920265
2	22.2	40.0	28.6	91.9	0881817786
3	90.5	12.3	21.7	85.7	1150262910
4	100	10.4	18.9	42.4	0992626050
5	83.3	2.9	5.6	59.7	0949250459
6	100	12.4	22.1	94.6	1151059737

Table 2: Results for the ToC Generation Task on the test set

3.1.5 Computing the PDF Page Numbers

Once the ToC is built, each header is associated to a page number. This page number refers to the print version. The PDF page number we have to submit is slightly different: a page shift may appear if the first page of the PDF is not "page 1". It is the case when the document contains a title page, which might be unnumbered, or includes preliminary pages which might also be not numbered or might use a different numbering alphabet.

In order to get the appropriate PDF page numbers, we choose to compute the shift between PDF page numbers and printed page numbers. In order to extract printed page numbers, we select a sample of PDF pages. We then look for a series of integers located at the same position on different pages. Once we found this series, we get the page shift by calculating the difference between the first printed page number of the series and its corresponding PDF page number.

3.1.6 Results and discussion

The official results of our system Daniel on the test set are given in table 1. The detailed results of our system are given in table 2. As expected, the system always has a good precision and a lower recall. We point out that low precision for book 2 is due to the fact that the ToC of the prospectus is more detailed than the ToC of the groundtruth.

Good precision and low recall are linked to our method which is based on locating and parsing the ToCs. ToCs does not reflect the true structure of the prospectuses. They are generally less detailed: lower level headers are not included. Moreover, if no ToC is present or found, the system relies on a simple fallback.

Due to lack of time for implementation, we only handled ToC located on one-column page layout, which is the most common case for this kind of document. We did not handle the difference of page format for odd and even pages. Simple improvements can be done to cover these two cases.

As said at the beginning of this section the main improvements would come from taking into account the whole content of the document. We did not have enough time to handle it properly. It would allow the handling of documents without ToC and would permit the extraction of titles that are not included in the ToC. It would be particularly useful for these financial documents where fine-grain subdivisions are present but not represented in the ToC.

3.2 Title Detection

The very first feature one can think about is the length of the segment, titles are shorter segments and are seldom longer than a line. The second feature that came to our mind is that titles are likely to be nonverbal sentences and in general exhibit a simpler syntactical structure. Other features like those provided with the dataset can be useful: begins with numbering, material aspect (bold/italic), capitalization (begin with capitals, all_caps). We advocate that these differences are related to style, therefore the different baselines and systems we propose rely on stylistic features. We used the basic set of features given with the dataset and we added three other types of features:

basic features : Provided in the dataset (Begins with Numbering, Is Bold, Is Italic, Is All Caps, begin With Cap, Page Number)

length The length of the segment in characters

stylo Relative frequency of each punctuation sign, numbers and capitalized letters

Our other approach relies on character based features, used in particular in autorship attribution (Brixtel, 2015). We chose character n-grams because of their simplicity to compute. We try different possible values of n: $n_{min} \leq n \leq n_{max}$ with all possible n_{min} and n_{max} values between 1 and 10 (and $n_{min} \leq n_{max}$). We computed a relative frequency for each n-gram in each example to

	Cross-valid	Test-set
B1 (basic features)	80.1	91.1
B2 (basic + length)	71.1	61.2
B3 (stylo)	75.5	87.6
B4 (stylo+basic)	72.2	84.2
B5 (stylo+length)	69.9	67.8
B6 (stylo+basic+length)	63.4	61.7
n-grams ($1 \leq n \leq 1$)	81.5	91.1
n-grams ($1 \leq n \leq 2$)	81.5	91.1
n-grams ($1 \leq n \leq 3$)	82.4	91.9
n-grams ($1 \leq n \leq 4$)	82.0	91.5
n-grams ($1 \leq n \leq 5$)	81.8	91.3

Table 3: Results for the title detection task for the Multinomial naive Bayes Classifier

	Cross-valid	Test-set
B1 (basic features)	83.2	92.9
B2 (basic + length)	85.4	93.6
B3 (stylo)	85.4	93.2
B4 (stylo+basic)	90.4	94.2
B5 (stylo+length)	90.0	93.7
B6 (stylo+basic+length)	90.6	**95.1**
n-grams ($1 \leq n \leq 1$)	94.0	94.6
n-grams ($1 \leq n \leq 2$)	94.2	94.5
n-grams ($1 \leq n \leq 3$)	94.3	94.8
n-grams ($1 \leq n \leq 4$)	93.5	**95.0**
n-grams ($1 \leq n \leq 5$)	93.1	95.1

Table 4: Results for the title detection task for the DT10 Decision Tree Classifier (in bold our two submissions)

classify in order to take into account their various size. In fact, with absolute frequencies the results were significantly worse. We will only report results obtained with the Multinomial Naive Bayes (MNB) and the DT10 classifier since other classifiers did not offer better results than the DT10. SVM (with linear and non-linear kernels) had difficulties to converge with our baseline features due to their insuffcient number.

In order to evaluate our methods and baselines we performed for each of them a ten-fold cross validation on the train set. The results on the train and test set are presented in Table 3 for the MNB classifier and Table 4 for the DT10 classifier. The first thing one can see is that the DT10 classifier outperforms the MNB in particular because the MNB classifier is not better with the stylometric features. The baselines with stylometric features worked well and our first submission was but the best method on the training data was the n-gram method (with $1 \leq n \leq 3$). However, we chose to submit the classifier trained with with $1 \leq n \leq 4$ because we believed it would be less prone to over-fitting. With $n_{min} > 1$ or $n_{max} > 5$ the results drop significantly.

What we did not expect is that our best baseline performed much better on the test-set and was even better than our other submission. However, it is very interesting result since our experiments on the train set seemed to show that 1-grams were sufficient to build a reasonably efficient classifier.

3.3 Results and Discussion

We showed that very simple features can be of great interest, in particular in cases of training data scarcity. The methods we proposed can be improved in two different directions, regarding the features exploitation or exploring other features regarding the style of titles VS the style of non-titles. First, for improving a character-based approach it seems that LSTM architectures can be of great interest. The second option would be to extract syntactic patterns since sentence structures are quite different in titles.

4 Conclusion

Title detection and Table of Content (ToC) extraction are two important tasks for Document Analysis, in particular in the context of digital libraries and scanned books.

We proposed two types of features for the Title Detection task, we used a naive Bayses classifier as a baseline and a decision tree (DT10). We showed that simple stylometric features (frequency of punctuation, numbers and capitalized letters) combined with visual characteristics (bold, italic. . .) achieve better results than the best character n-gram approach (1-4 grams). Although this system did not achieved state-of-the-art performances, the results shows that simple and easy-to-compute features can provide very reliable results.

Regarding the ToC Extraction task, we choose to extract the structure from the ToC of the prospectuses. We are pleased to see that are our expectations are confirmed. Our system obtains a good precision and lower recall. For a next edition, we would like to focus on the extraction of the structure from the whole document content.

References

Ali Ait Elhadj, Mohand Boughanem, Mohamed Mezghiche, and Fatiha Souam. 2012. Using structural similarity for clustering XML documents. *Knowledge and Information Systems*, 32(1):109–139.

Juliàn Alarte, Josep Silva, and Salvador Tamarit. 2019. What web template extractor should i use? a benchmarking and comparison for five template extractors. *ACM Trans. Web*, 13(2):9:1–9:19.

Joeran Beel, Stefan Langer, Marcel Genzmehr, and Christoph Müller. 2013. Docear's pdf inspector: Title extraction from pdf files. In *Proceedings of the 13th ACM/IEEE-CS Joint Conference on Digital Libraries*, JCDL '13, pages 443–444, New York, NY, USA. ACM.

Romain Brixtel. 2015. Maximal repeats enhance substring-based authorship attribution. In *Proceedings of the International Conference Recent Advances in Natural Language Processing*, pages 63–71, Hissar, Bulgaria. INCOMA Ltd. Shoumen, BULGARIA.

Rik de Busser and Marie-Francine Moens. 2006. *Information extraction and information technology*, pages 1–22. Springer, Berlin, Heidelberg.

Sahar Changuel, Nicolas Labroche, and Bernadette Bouchon-Meunier. 2009. A general learning method for automatic titleextraction from html pages. In *Machine Learning and Data Mining in Pattern Recognition*, pages 704–718, Berlin, Heidelberg. Springer Berlin Heidelberg.

Béatrice Daille, Evelyne Jacquey, Gaël Lejeune, Luis Felipe Melo, and Yannick Toussaint. 2016. Ambiguity Diagnosis for Terms in Digital Humanities. In *Language Resources and Evaluation Conference*, Portorož, Slovenia.

Hervé Déjean. 2007. *pdf2xml open source software*. Last access on July 31, 2019.

Misha Denil, Alban Demiraj, and Nando de Freitas. 2014. Extraction of salient sentences from labelled documents. *CoRR*, abs/1412.6815.

Antoine Doucet, Gabriella Kazai, Sebastian Colutto, and Günter Mühlberger. 2013. Overview of the ICDAR 2013 Competition on Book Structure Extraction. In *Proc. of the 12th International Conference on Document Analysis and Recognition (ICDAR'2013)*, pages 1438–1443, Washington DC, USA.

Antoine Doucet and Miro Lehtonen. 2007. Unsupervised classification of text-centric xml document collections. In *Comparative Evaluation of XML Information Retrieval Systems, 5th International Workshop of the Initiative for the Evaluation of XML Retrieval, INEX*, volume 4518 of *Lecture Notes in Computer Science*, pages 497–509. Springer.

Emmanuel Giguet, Alexandre Baudrillart, and Nadine Lucas. 2009. Resurgence for the book structure extraction competition. In *INEX 2009 Workshop Pre-Proceedings*, pages 136–142.

Emmanuel Giguet and Nadine Lucas. 2010a. The book structure extraction competition with the resurgence software at caen university. In *Focused Retrieval and Evaluation*, pages 170–178, Berlin, Heidelberg. Springer Berlin Heidelberg.

Emmanuel Giguet and Nadine Lucas. 2010b. The book structure extraction competition with the resurgence software for part and chapter detection at caen university. In *Comparative Evaluation of Focused Retrieval - 9th International Workshop INEX, Vugh, The Netherlands, Revised Selected Papers*, volume 6932 of *Lecture Notes in Computer Science*, pages 128–139. Springer.

Silja Huttunen, Arto Vihavainen, Peter von Etter, and Roman Yangarber. 2011. Relevance prediction in information extraction using discourse and lexical features. In *Proceedings of the 18th Nordic Conference of Computational Linguistics (NODALIDA 2011)*, pages 114–121.

Stefan Klampfl, Michael Granitzer, Kris Jack, and Roman Kern. 2014. Unsupervised document structure analysis of digital scientific articles. *Int. J. Digit. Libr.*, 14(3-4):83–99.

Gaël Lejeune, Romain Brixtel, Antoine Doucet, and Nadine Lucas. 2015. Multilingual event extraction for epidemic detection. *Artificial Intelligence in Medicine*, 65(2):131 – 143. Intelligent healthcare informatics in big data era.

Gaël Lejeune and Lichao Zhu. 2018. A new proposal for evaluating web page cleaning tools. *Computación y Sistemas*, 22(4).

Thi-Tuyet-Hai Nguyen, Antoine Doucet, and Mickael Coustaty. 2017. Enhancing table of contents extraction by system aggregation. In *2017 14th IAPR International Conference on Document Analysis and Recognition (ICDAR)*, volume 01, pages 242–247.

Sira Ferradans Rémi Juge, Najah-Imane Bentabet. 2019. The fintoc-2019 shared task: Financial document structure extraction. In *The Second Workshop on Financial Narrative Processing of NoDalida 2019*.

Dominika Tkaczyk, Andrew Collins, and Joeran Beel. 2018. Who did what?: Identifying author contributions in biomedical publications using naïve bayes. In *Proceedings of the 18th ACM/IEEE on Joint Conference on Digital Libraries*, JCDL '18, pages 387–388, New York, NY, USA. ACM.

Yewei Xue, Yunhua Hu, Guomao Xin, Ruihua Song, Shuming Shi, Yunbo Cao, Chin-Yew Lin, and Hang Li. 2007. Web page title extraction and its application. *Information Processing & Management*, 43(5):1332 – 1347. Patent Processing.

FinDSE@FinTOC-2019 Shared Task

Carla Abreu[1,2], **Henrique Lopes Cardoso**[1,2], **Eugénio Oliveira**[1,2]
Faculdade de Engenharia da Universidade do Porto[1], LIACC[2]
Rua Dr. Roberto Frias, s/n, Porto, Portugal
(ei08165, hlc, eco)@fe.up.pt

Abstract

We present the approach developed at the Faculty of Engineering of the University of Porto to participate in FinTOC-2019 Financial Document Structure Extraction – Detection of titles sub-task. Several financial documents are produced in machine-readable format. Due to the poor structure of these documents, it is an arduous task to retrieve the desired information from them. The aim of this sub-task is to detect titles in this kind of documents. We propose a supervised learning approach making use of linguistic, semantic and morphological features to classify a text block as title or non title. The proposed methodology got a F1 score of 97.01%.

1 Introduction

Several financial documents are produced, every day, for different financial applications. Some of these documents are mandatory by law, however they are not created following the same standard and sometimes have a poor structure, making it difficult to retrieve the desired information. These documents are usually published in machine-readable format (such as Portable Document Format (PDF) files) but unfortunately, they remain untagged – they have no tags for identifying layout items such as paragraphs, columns, or tables. Document structuring has clear benefits to users, enabling them to gain direct access to the relevant part of the document (which can be lengthy), improving also search performance.

Financial Prospectuses are financial documents where investment funds are described, and have a non-standard content format. These documents need to be consulted by distinct persons and fast retrievals of data are desired.

A lot of effort has already been put to label the structure of documents. Some known projects are the Million Book project (Linke, 2003), the Open Content Alliance (OCA) (Suber, 2005), or the digitisation of Google (Coyle, 2006) (Doucet et al., 2011). Projects that have aim at automatically recognizing document structure take, as input, a document in PDF format, or its content obtained via Optical Character Recognition (OCR).

Document structure extraction is a well studied problem in document analysis, and has been applied in distinct types of documents and in different domains. Works on this matter go from scientific articles (Klampfl et al., 2014) (Bast and Korzen, 2017) to books (Linke, 2003).

Rangoni et al. (Rangoni et al., 2012) make use of three types of features: geometrical (width, height, X position, among others), morphological (the font and other characteristics, such as italics, bold, and so on) and semantic (language, is numeric, and so on). Bitew (Bitew, 2018) also includes three distinct categories: textual features (similar to semantic), markup features (similar to morphological) and linguistic (related with Part of Speech). As described, some authors groups features in categories; however, some studies use only one category, including Kim et al. (Kim et al., 2017), who make use of morphological elements only for logical structured extraction.

The methodologies used to address this problem include rule-based and machine learning approaches (Klampfl and Kern, 2013) (He, 2017).

In this paper we present a supervised approach to automatically classify a text block as title or non title (a binary classification problem), making use of linguistic, semantic and morphological features. In Section 2, we describe the FinTOC Sub-Task on title detection, and in Section 3 we analyze the provided data. In Section 4 we present our approach, followed by the experimental setup in Section 5. Results are discussed in Section 6. In Section 7 we conclude.

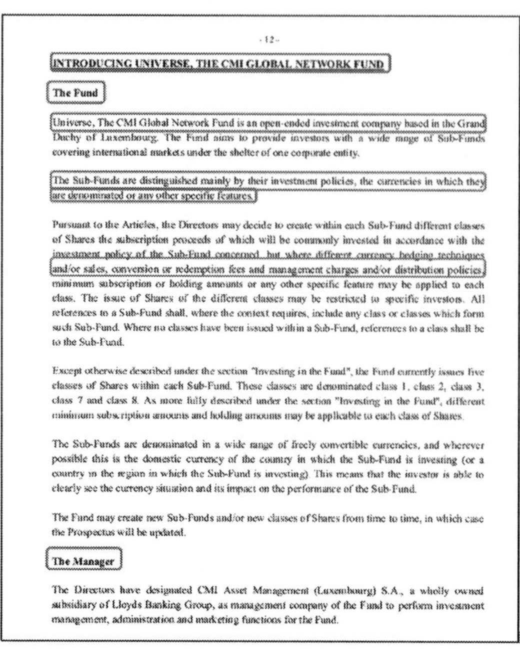

Figure 1: Financial Prospectuses document layout

2 Sub-Task Description

The task addressed in this work concerns the detection of titles in financial prospectuses (Rémi Juge, 2019). Given a set of text blocks, the goal is to classify each given text block as a 'title' or 'non-title'. As shown in Figure 1[1], titles can have different layouts (marked with red and green boxes), and they have to be distinguished from regular text ('non-title' marked with grey boxes).

The evaluation metric used in the task is the F1 metric.

3 Dataset

FinTOC organizers provide an excel file with text blocks information. Each line represents one text block and each column their characteristics:

- *text blocks*: text block textual content;

- *begins_with_numbering*: 1 if the text block begins with a numbering such as 1., A/, b), III., etc. . . .; 0 otherwise;

- *is_bold*: 1 if the text block appears in bold in the PDF document; 0 otherwise;

- *is_italic*: 1 if the text block is in italic in the pdf document; 0 otherwise;

	Title	Non Title
Excel - Number of Rows	2,420	13,092
Average of NC / TB	25.03	152.82
Standard Deviation of NC / TB	14.87	300.87
Variance of NC / TB	221	90,525.25
Min of NC / TB	2	1
Max of NC / TB	143	7,715

Table 1: Training set statistics (TB = text block; NC = number of characters).

- *is_all_caps*: 1 if the text block is all composed of capital letters; 0 otherwise;

- *begins_with_cap*: 1 if the text block begins with a capital letter; 0 otherwise;

- *xmlfile*: the xmlfile from which the above features have been derived;

- *page_nb*: the page number in the PDF where the text bock appears;

- *label*: 1 if text block is a title, 0 otherwise.

The test set has the same format as the training set, but without information in the last column of the CSV file. This column is meant to be filled in by systems participating in the task.

The training set contains 44 distinct documents, not standardized. The CSV file used as training set contains 75625 annotated rows. More details about the training set are included on Table 1 and Table 2.

The test set is composed of 7 PDF files (whose length ranges from 35 to 134 pages, with an average of 64 pages). The CSV file is composed of 14816 non-annotated rows.

4 Proposed approach

4.1 Features

Text blocks are provided with some characteristics, such as: (Fe1) begins_with_numbering; (Fe2) is_bold; (Fe3) is_italic; (Fe4) is_all_caps; and (Fe5) begins_with_cap. These elements are described in Section 3.

We have extracted additional features from the text block, as follows:

- (Fe6) Number of characters;
- (Fe6a) Number of characters distributed in categories (Table 2) ;
- (Fe7) First block character type: alphabetic upper/lower, numeric, other (space or punctuation);

[1]FNP Workhop Series – Title detection subtask: http://wp.lancs.ac.uk/cfie/shared-task/

$ID_{Category}$	Range	TS_{Title}	$TS_{NonTitle}$
0	0	0	0
1	1 - 3	2	334
2	4 - 9	80	48
3	10 - 16	695	203
4	17 - 21	553	160
5	22 - 30	400	87
6	31 - 40	366	73
7	41 - 50	164	48
8	51 - 70	129	108
9	71 - 100	23	157
10	101 - 150	8	178
11	151 - 200	0	181
12	201 - 400	0	523
13	401 - 600	0	172
14	601 - 1000	0	114
15	1001 - 1500	0	30
16	>1501	0	4

Table 2: Number of characters distributed in categories and in the training set (TS)

- (Fe8) Last block character type: alphabetic upper/lower, numeric, other (space or punctuation);
- (Fe9) Number of tokens;
- (Fe10) Number of sentences contained in the block text;
- (Fe11) Part Of Speech of the first token in the block text;
- (Fe12) Contains date;
- (Fe13) Title suggestion word - if the first token belongs to one of these words: 'appendix', 'annex', and others;
- (Fe14) Tense block - check if the text block is written in the past, present or future.

The enunciated features belong to three different types: morphological (Fe2, Fe3, Fe4, Fe5, Fe6, Fe6a, Fe7, Fe8), semantic (Fe1, Fe12), and linguistic (Fe11, Fe13, Fe14). Tense, part of speech, title suggestion words and contains date are language dependent features applied only to English language.

4.2 Classification Algorithms

Supervised learning techniques create a model that predicts the value of a target variable based on a set of input variables. One challenge is to select the most appropriate algorithm for the task of classifying as 'title' or 'non-title' a given text block. We have compared the following algorithms: Decision Tree (DT), Extra-tree classifier (EXT), and Gradient Boosting (GBC).

As shown in Table 3, different configurations were attempted for each algorithm. Implementations of these algorithms are provided by the

Alg_{ID}	**Algorithm**	**Configuration**
DT_1	DT	random_state=0
DTC_1	DT	max_depth=None min_samples_split=2 random_state=0
EXT_1	EXT	n_estimators=10 max_depth=None min_samples_split=2 random_state=0
GBC_1	GBC	loss='exponential'
GBC_2	GBC	n_estimators=2000 learning_rate=0.75 max_depth=5

Table 3: List of algorithm configurations

	E_1	E_2	E_3	E_4	E_5
Fe1	x	x	x		x
Fe2	x	x	x	x	x
Fe3	x	x			x
Fe4	x	x	x		x
Fe5	x	x	x		x
Fe6		x	x	x	
Fe6a	x				
Fe7	x	x	x		
Fe8	x	x	x	x	
Fe9	x	x	x	x	
Fe10	x	x	x		
Fe11	x	x	x	x	
Fe12		x	x		
Fe13		x			
Fe14		x			

Table 4: List of features used in each experimental setup.

Python library scikit-learn library[2].

5 Experimental Setup

The set of features used in each experimental setup is shown in Table 4. Experiment 5 (E_5) is our baseline, as this setup includes all the features available in the dataset. We combine all the available features with all extracted by us in Experiment 2 (E_2). We create a model based on E_2 and select all the features with an importance above 0.03 to compose Experiment 3 (E_3) and above 0.07 to include in Experiment 4 (E_4).

Experiment 1 (E_1) was based in our analysis regarding text blocks number of characters categories distribution, such as presented in Table 2.

6 Experimental Evaluation

Several combinations of features (Table 4) and algorithms (Table 3) were applied to solve the title classification problem. The results obtained are shown in Table 5.

---

[2]sklearn: https://scikit-learn.org

Exp	Alg_ID	TN	FP	FN	TP	F1_title	F1_non
E_1	DT_1	18,882	756	705	2,345	76.25	96.28
E_1	DTC_1	18,882	756	705	2345	76,25	96,28
E_1	EXT_1	**18,932**	**706**	**684**	**2,366**	**77.30**	**96.46**
E_1	GBC_1	*14,954*	*4,684*	**629**	**2,421**	47.68	84.92
E_1	GBC_2	18,829	809	1,192	1,858	65.00	94.95
E_2	DT_1	18,851	787	747	2,303	75.02	96.09
E_2	DTC_1	18,851	787	747	2,303	75.02	96.09
E_2	EXT_1	18,891	747	741	2,309	75.63	96.21
E_2	GBC_1	18,856	782	737	2,313	75.28	96.13
E_2	GBC_2	18,816	822	1,214	1,836	64.33	94.87
E_3	DT_1	18,850	788	794	2,256	74.04	95.97
E_3	DTC_1	18,850	788	794	2,256	74.04	95.97
E_3	EXT_1	18,880	758	786	2,264	74.57	96.07
E_3	GBC_1	18,735	903	770	2,280	73.16	95.73
E_3	GBC_2	18,813	825	1,225	1,825	64.04	94.83
E_4	DT_1	18,801	837	848	2,202	72.33	95.71
E_4	DTC_1	18,801	837	848	2,202	72.33	95.71
E_4	EXT_1	18,810	828	847	2,203	72.46	95.74
E_4	GBC_1	18,798	840	877	2,173	71.68	95.63
E_4	GBC_2	18,739	899	1,208	1,842	63.62	94.68
E_5	DT_1	**19,280**	**358**	*2,328*	*722*	34.96	93.49
E_5	DTC_1	**19,280**	**358**	*2,328*	*722*	34.96	93.49
E_5	EXT_1	**19,280**	**358**	*2,328*	*722*	34.96	93.49
E_5	GBC_1	**19,280**	**358**	*2,328*	*722*	34.96	93.49
E_5	GBC_2	**19,280**	**358**	*2,329*	*721*	34.96	93.49

Table 5: Results

E_5 is the experiment that has as feature set all the features available upfront with the dataset. This experiment got similar results using distinct supervised learning algorithms. The results obtained indicate that this set of features are not enough to classify block text titles, showing a high number of false negatives and a low number of true positives.

The DT_1 and DTC_1 algorithms have distinct configurations, however they presented the same results when exposed to the same feature set. The GBC_1 algorithm configuration was more sensible when exposed to a specific feature set – in E_1, this algorithm has shown the higher number of false positives obtained in our experiments. GBC_2 was the worst configuration algorithm used in this classification, having the lowest value of true positives.

The feature set used in E_1 includes all features provided by the competition organizers. Other features were added, some of them related to how the text appears in the text block (such as number of characters or sentences), and also language dependent features (such as the case of F11). Except for GBC_1, all other algorithm configurations reached their best result. EXT_1 got the best performance in the task of title classification.

FinTOC-2019 received two submissions for each participant, on which we achieved F1 score of 97.01% on E_1 with EXT_1 reaching the fifth position and the sixth position with F1 score of 96.84% on E_1 with DT_1.

7 Conclusion

It is difficult to retrieve the desired information from lengthy documents when the Table Of Content (TOC) is missing. TOC helps the reader to identify what is written in each section, enabling an oriented reading. The aim of this study is to classify each text block into title or non-title, a step towards identifying each section in a document.

In this work we propose a supervised learning strategy to classify text blocks. We also proposed an extension of the provided feature set based on recognizing new characteristics of text blocks (related with the text block composition and the use of linguistic resources). The dataset available in this competition was composed by five features. We experimented the use of these features but the results obtained point out that these are not enough to the envisaged classification task.

We recognize more features in text blocks, some of them related with the text composition and others related with linguistic resources. Not all of these features have shown to be essential for title classification.

Title detection got an high performance using Extra-Tree classifier with the following features: the five ones available on the dataset (*begings_with_numbering*, *is_bold*, *is_italic*, *is_all_caps*, *begin_with_cap*) and six more (number of characters, first sentence character, last sentence character, number of tokens, number of sentences, Part of speech of the first sentence element).

References

Hannah Bast and Claudius Korzen. 2017. A benchmark and evaluation for text extraction from pdf. In *Proceedings of the 17th ACM/IEEE Joint Conference on Digital Libraries*, pages 99–108. IEEE Press.

Semere Kiros Bitew. 2018. Logical structure extraction of electronic documents using contextual information. Master's thesis, University of Twente.

Karen Coyle. 2006. Mass digitization of books. *The Journal of Academic Librarianship*, 32(6):641–645.

Antoine Doucet, Gabriella Kazai, and Jean-Luc Meunier. 2011. Icdar 2011 book structure extraction competition. In *2011 International Conference on Document Analysis and Recognition*, pages 1501–1505. IEEE.

Yi He. 2017. Extracting document structure of a text with visual and textual cues. Master's thesis, University of Twente.

Tae-young Kim, Suntae Kim, Sangchul Choi, Jeong-Ah Kim, Jae-Young Choi, Jong-Won Ko, Jee-Huong Lee, and Youngwha Cho. 2017. A machine-learning based approach for extracting logical structure of a styled document. *TIIS*, 11(2):1043–1056.

Stefan Klampfl, Michael Granitzer, Kris Jack, and Roman Kern. 2014. Unsupervised document structure analysis of digital scientific articles. *International journal on digital libraries*, 14(3-4):83–99.

Stefan Klampfl and Roman Kern. 2013. An unsupervised machine learning approach to body text and table of contents extraction from digital scientific articles. In *International Conference on Theory and Practice of Digital Libraries*, pages 144–155. Springer.

Erika C Linke. 2003. Million book project. *Encyclopedia of Library and Information Science: Lib-Pub*, page 1889.

Yves Rangoni, Abdel Belaïd, and Szilárd Vajda. 2012. Labelling logical structures of document images using a dynamic perceptive neural network. *International Journal on Document Analysis and Recognition (IJDAR)*, 15(1):45–55.

Sira Ferradans Rémi Juge, Najah-Imane Bentabet. 2019. The fintoc-2019 shared task: Financial document structure extraction. In *The Second Workshop on Financial Narrative Processing of NoDalida 2019*.

Peter Suber. 2005. The open content alliance. *SPARC Open Access Newsletter*.

UWB@FinTOC-2019 Shared Task: Financial Document Title Detection

Tomáš Hercig
NTIS – New Technologies
for the Information Society,
Faculty of Applied Sciences,
University of West Bohemia,
Technická 8, 306 14 Plzeň
Czech Republic
`tigi@kiv.zcu.cz`

Pavel Král
Department of Computer
Science and Engineering,
Faculty of Applied Sciences
University of West Bohemia,
Univerzitní 8, 306 14 Plzeň
Czech Republic
`pkral@kiv.zcu.cz`

Abstract

This paper describes our system created for the Financial Document Structure Extraction Shared Task (FinTOC-2019) Task A: Title Detection. We rely on the XML representation of the financial prospectuses for additional layout information about the text (font type, font size, etc.). Our constrained system uses only the provided training data without any additional external resources. Our system is based on the Maximum Entropy classifier and various features including font type and font size. Our system achieves F1 score 97.2% and is ranked #3 among 10 submitted systems.

1 Introduction

Financial documents are used to report activities, financial situation, investment plans, and operational information to shareholders, investors, and financial markets. These reports are usually created on an annual basis in machine-readable formats often only with minimal structure information.

The goal of the Financial Document Structure Extraction Shared Task (FinTOC-2019) (Juge et al., 2019) is to analyse these financial prospectuses[1] and automatically extract their structure similarly to Doucet et al. (2013).

The majority of prospectuses are published without a table of content (TOC), which is usually needed to help readers navigate within the document.

2 Task

The goal of FinTOC-2019 shared task is to extract the table of content from the financial prospectuses. The shared task consists of two subtasks:

- Subtask A classifies given text blocks as titles or non-titles.

- Subtask B organizes provided headers into a hierarchical table of content.

We participated only in subtask A. For additional information (e.g. about subtask B) see the task description paper (Juge et al., 2019).

Systems participating in this shared task were given a sample collection of financial prospectuses with different level of structure and different lengths as training data.

We approached the title detection subtask as a binary classification task. For all experiments we use Maximum Entropy classifier with default settings from Brainy machine learning library (Konkol, 2014).

Data statistics for the title detection subtask are shown in Table 1.

Label	Test	Train
Non-title	13 928 (94.0%)	65 354 (86.4%)
Title	888 (6.0%)	10 271 (13.6%)

Table 1: Data statistics for Subtask A.

3 Dataset

The provided training collection of documents contains:

- PDF format of the documents

- XML representation of the PDFs as given by the Poppler utility libraries; this representation contains the text of the documents as well as layout information about the text (font, bold, italic, and coordinates).

- CSV file with gold labels.

---

[1] Official PDF documents in which investment funds precisely describe their characteristics and investment modalities.

Label	Test	Fixed Test	Train	Fixed Train
Non-title	13 928	12 844 (92.2%)*	65 354	60 533 (92.6%)
Title	888	821 (92.5%)*	10 271	10 209 (99.4%)
Sum	14 816	13 665 (92.2%)	75 625	70 742 (93.5%)

Table 2: Comparison of datasets with fixed issues.

The XML file consists of page elements and has essentially the following structure:

```
<page number="1" ...>
<fontspec id="0" size="11"
family="Times" color="#000000"/>
<fontspec id="1" size="9".../>
<text ...><b> </b></text>
<text ...>Man Umbrella SICAV </text>
...
</page>
...
```

The CSV file contains the following fields delimited by tabs. For more details see the task description paper (Juge et al., 2019).

- Text blocks: a list of strings computed by a heuristic algorithm; the algorithm segments the documents into homogeneous text regions according to given rules

- Begins_with_numbering: 1 if the text block begins with a numbering such as 1., A/, b), III., etc.; 0 otherwise

- Is_bold: 1 if the title appear in bold in the PDF document; 0 otherwise

- Is_italic: 1 if the title is in italic in the PDF document; 0 otherwise

- Is_all_caps: 1 if the title is all composed of capital letters; 0 otherwise

- Begins_with_cap: 1 if the title begins with a capital letter; 0 otherwise

- Xmlfile: the XML file from which the above features have been derived

- Page_nb: the page number in the PDF where the text block appears

- Label: 1 if text line is a title, 0 otherwise

According to the organizers, participants can either use the segmentation into text blocks suggested in the CSV file provided for the subtask A, or come up with their own segmentation algorithm which is highly encouraged.

We decided to use the XML file and thus needed to link the annotation labels to the original XML text representation.

4   Issues

We mentioned in previous section that the segmentation into text blocks is provided in the CSV file. However, that means that we need to find the mapping from the annotated text segments onto the original XML text representation.

We wrote an algorithm that goes through both files and tries to find the best mapping on a given page assuming the annotated text from the CSV file appears in the same order of occurrence as the text in the XML file. Unfortunately, that is not always true, thus we decided to modify the training CSV file and fix the issues, described in the following sections, that caused our algorithm to fail. We fixed only the necessary part of the dataset in order for our algorithm to work. The scale of these issues is illustrated in Table 2.

The percentage ratio in Table 2 is between the original and the fixed dataset. The star sign indicates that the labels were not known at the time and thus the issue described in Section 4.1 only eliminated duplicates not taking into consideration the assigned label, leading to the removal of more title labels compared to the train dataset.

The algorithm mentioned at the beginning of this section maps up to N text blocks from the XML file to one annotation. This is basically the reverse process to the one constructing the text blocks for the CSV file. We use the first matching text segment from the XML file to assign the font and other meta-information to the annotations.

The following example is the XML file text blocks that can be mapped to the example in Section 4.2.

```
<text ...><b>4. Stock exchange listing
</b></text>
<text ...>The Sub-Fund ... </text>
<text ...>Details regarding ...
... Multi-Strategy. </text>
<text ...><b>5.   Shares </b></text>
```

4.1 Duplicate Entries

When we found a duplicate entry in the CSV file we removed the duplicity leaving only one occurrence of the text according to the original PDF. If the duplicate entries varied in the gold label we usually left the label indicating title.

In the following example we added the line number from the original CSV file delimited by colon and shortened the XML file name.

```
20139: General Meeting 0 0 0 0 1
 LU..._ManConvertibles.xml 24 1
20140: General Meeting 0 0 0 0 1
 LU..._ManConvertibles.xml 24 0
```

4.2 Wrong Order of Occurrence

The CSV file contains repetitions[2] of data causing our mapping algorithm to fail on the given page because of the wrong order of text occurrence. We corrected the repetitions leaving only one occurrence of the text according to the original PDF. If the duplicate entries varied in the gold label we usually left the label indicating title.

In the following example we added the line number from the original CSV file delimited by colon and left out the text characteristics, XML file name (`LU..._ManConvertibles.xml`), the page number (120), and parts of the texts as they are unnecessary. The bold text denotes the fixed version of the annotations.

```
21782:3. Currency ... 1
21783:The reference currency ...
 cannot be excluded. ... 0
21784:4. Stock exchange listing ... 1
21785:The Sub-Fund may apply ...
 Multi-Strategy. ... 1
21786:5. Shares ... 0
21787:The Sub-Fund shall ...
 Sub-Fund. ... 0
21788:6. Share classes ... 1
21789:General ... 1
21790:3. Currency ... 0
21791:The reference currency ...
 cannot be excluded. ... 0
21792:4. Stock exchange listing ... 0
21793:The Sub-Fund may apply ...
 Multi-Strategy. ... 0
21794:5. Shares ... 0
21795:The Sub-Fund shall ...
 Sub-Fund. ... 0
21796:6. Share classes General ... 0
```

4.3 Missing Text Beginning

In rare cases the beginning of annotated text from the CSV file was missing. We fixed the cases our algorithm discovered. See the example that occurred on line 21782 for XML file (`LU...ControlPFCo.xml`) below.

```
original:SUBSCRIPTIONS ...
fixed:(5) SUBSCRIPTIONS ...
```

---

² We did not found these repetitions in the original PDF files nor in the XML files.

5 Features

We tried to create the best feature set using all the provided meta-information. The following features proved useful and were used in our submissions.

- **Character n-grams (ChN$_n$):** Separate feature for each n-gram representing the n-gram presence in the text. We do it separately for different orders $n \in \{1, 2\}$ and remove n-gram with frequency $f \leq 2$.

- **Binary Features (B):** We use separate binary feature for all five text characteristics from the CSV file (Begins_with_numbering, Is_bold, Is_italic, Is_all_caps, and Begins_with_cap).

- **First Orto-characters (FO):** Bag of first three orthographic[3] characters with at least 2 occurrences.

- **Last Orto-characters (LO):** Bag of last three orthographic[3] characters with at least 2 occurrences.

- **Font Size (FS):** We map the font size of text into a one-hot vector with length ten and use this vector as features for the classifier. The frequency belongs to one of ten equal-frequency bins[4]. Each bin corresponds to a position in the vector. We remove font sizes with frequency ≤ 2.

- **Font Type Size (FTS):** For each font type we map the text length into a one-hot vector with length five and use this vector as features for the classifier. The frequency belongs to one of five equal-frequency bins[5]. Each bin corresponds to a position in the vector.

- **Text Length (TL):** We map the text length into a one-hot vector with length ten and use this vector as features for the classifier. The frequency belongs to one of ten equal-frequency bins[4]. Each bin corresponds to a position in the vector. We remove text lengths with frequency ≤ 2.

---

³ All lower cased letters were replaced by "a", upper cased letters by "A" and digits by "1" (e.g. "Char3" = "Aaaa1").

⁴ The frequencies from the training data are split into ten equal-size bins according to 10% quantiles.

⁵ The frequencies from the training data are split into five equal-size bins according to 20% quantiles.

6 Results

The results in Table 4 show our ranking in the FinTOC-2019 shared task using the original dataset.

Our submission UWB 1 was achieved using probability threshold $t = 0.8$ for the classifiers' predictions. The submission UWB 2 was achieved using the default threshold of $t = 0.5$.

Both submissions were outputs of our model trained on the fixed dataset and contained the fixed and the original test set.

For the original test data we used the predictions of our model trained on the fixed test file. Then the removed lines / labels from the original dataset were automatically matched to the fixed dataset and if an exact match was found for a predicted title we marked the removed line in the original test set as a title.

Our submissions and the fixed train / test datasets are available for research purposes at `https://gitlab.com/tigi.cz/fintoc-2019`.

We performed ablation experiments to illustrate which features are the most beneficial using the default threshold $t = 0.5$ (see Table 3). Numbers represent the performance change when the given feature is removed (i.e. lower number means better feature). We used approximately 20% of the fixed training dataset[6] for evaluation and we used the rest of the dataset for training the features. Our evaluation includes accuracy and macro-averaged F1-score which is slightly different from the task evaluation metric: weighted F1-score (see the python evaluation script provided by organizers).

We can see that all features are beneficial for the results. The most helpful features apart from character n-grams include binary features representing provided text characteristics from the CSV file, first orto-characters, and font size.

Detailed statistical analysis into the datasets and either cross-validation or gold labels for the test set would be needed in order to infer further, more accurate, insides.

7 Conclusion

In this paper we described our UWB system participating in FinTOC 2019 shared task for financial document title detection.

---

[6]We used all annotations for five XML files.

Feature	Accuracy	F1-macro
ALL*	96.42%	94.07%
ChN $_1$	-0.60%	-1.08%
ChN $_2$	-3.88%	-7.52%
B	-1.69%	-2.23%
FO	-0.50%	-0.68%
LO	-0.30%	-0.31%
FS	-0.45%	-0.50%
FTS	-0.10%	-0.07%
TL	-0.13%	-0.06%

* Using all features in the ablation study.

Table 3: Feature ablation study.

Team	Submission	F1-weighted
Aiai	2	98.19%
Aiai	1	97.66%
UWB	2	97.24%
YseopLab	2	97.16%
FinDSE	1	97.01%
FinDSE	2	96.84%
UWB	1	96.53%
Daniel	1	94.88%
Daniel	2	94.17%
YseopLab	1	93.19%

Table 4: Results for Subtask A.

Our best results have been achieved by Maximum Entropy classifier combining available metadata, such as font type and font size, by careful feature engineering. Our system is ranked #3 among 10 participating systems' submissions.

Acknowledgments

This publication was supported by the project LO1506 of the Czech Ministry of Education, Youth and Sports under the program NPU I.

References

A. Doucet, G. Kazai, S. Colutto, and G. Mhlberger. 2013. ICDAR 2013 Competition on Book Structure Extraction. In *2013 12th International Conference on Document Analysis and Recognition*, pages 1438–1443.

Rémi Juge, Najah-Imane Bentabet, and Sira Ferradans. 2019. The FinTOC-2019 Shared Task: Financial Document Structure Extraction. In *The Second Workshop on Financial Narrative Processing of NoDalida 2019*.

Michal Konkol. 2014. Brainy: A Machine Learning Library. In Leszek Rutkowski, Marcin Korytkowski, Rafal Scherer, Ryszard Tadeusiewicz, Lotfi Zadeh, and Jacek Zurada, editors, *Artificial Intelligence and Soft Computing*, volume 8468 of *Lecture Notes in Computer Science*, pages 490–499. Springer International Publishing.

Association for Computational Linguistics
209 N. Eighth Street
Stroudsburg, Pennsylvania 18360

ISBN 978-1-5108-9441-9